BAYOU SARA

—*Used To Be*

BAYOU SARA

SARA

—Used To Be

Anne Butler & Helen Williams

2017

University of Louisiana at Lafayette Press

On the cover are three photographs of nineteenth-century Bayou Sara, courtesy of the West Feliciana Historical Society.

The painting *Moon River*, by gifted artist Michael Blaser, shows the Anchor Line packet steamers *Bayou Sara* and *Belle Memphis* that epitomized the great antebellum steamboats; all Anchor Line vessels were named for cities along the river. Blaser calls himself "Painter of the Rivers, Lakes and Deep Water." He complements his coveted limited-edition series of canvas giclees and lithographs with fascinating and well-researched river lore. Look for his homepage online to see more of his wonderful works.

ISBN 13 (paper): 978-1-946160-00-3
http://ulpress.org
University of Louisiana at Lafayette Press
P.O. Box 43558
Lafayette, LA 70504-3558
Printed on acid-free pape

Library of Congress Cataloging-in-Publication Data

Names: Butler, Anne, 1944- author. | Williams, Helen, 1936- author.
Title: Bayou Sara : --used to be / Anne Butler & Helen Williams.
Description: Lafayette, LA : University of Louisiana at Lafayette Press, 2017.
Identifiers: LCCN 2017002322 | ISBN 9781946160003 (alk. paper)
Subjects: LCSH: Bayou Sara (La.)--History. | Harbors--Louisiana--Bayou
Sara--History--19th century.
Classification: LCC F379.B38 B88 2017 | DDC 976.3/17--dc23
LC record available at https://lccn.loc.gov/2017002322

Table of Contents

Bayou Sara layout with all the squares numbered, completed by surveyor W.B. Smith, ca. 1893. Courtesy of the West Feliciana Historical Society.

Introduction

The steamboats still dock at Bayou Sara, just as they did in the nineteenth century when it was the most important port on the Mississippi River between New Orleans and Natchez, its riverfront crowded with wharves, warehouses, and the offices of commission merchants. But where once there was the bustle of commerce and the noisy gaiety of life, today there are only thick stands of cottonwood trees and weeping willows.

In the absence of levees, the river floodwaters still wash the site most springtimes and sometimes cover the access road from St. Francisville—a poignant reminder of the river's power and of the price early residents paid for the convenience of living right along what was the area's primary transportation route in the early nineteenth century.

Who were these residents, so resilient as to return year after year and sweep out the floodwaters and start their lives all over again? Where did they come from? And why did they come? Why did they stay?

1

The Early Years

In the 1700s, flatboaters transporting loads of produce and other goods from along the Ohio River Valley would float down the Mississippi River and often pull into the calm waters of Bayou Sara creek to spend the night out of the river's swift currents. Sometimes they would unload their wares onto smaller vessels capable of going up the creek to the plantations along its shores; other times they would continue on to New Orleans, where the goods were sold and the boats were broken up and sold for lumber, leaving the boatmen to return on foot upriver to wherever they had come from.

By the late eighteenth century, a little settlement sprang up where Bayou Sara creek emptied into the Mississippi River, taking its name from the creek. And where did the creek get *its* name? Stories vary. Early written accounts, including historical quarterly articles by Miss Louise Butler of the Cottage Plantation near St. Francisville, attribute the name of the stream to an old woman named Sara who lived at its mouth and washed her clothes in its waters. This may or may not be so, but the name Bayou Sara blessedly took precedence over previous designations for the stream on early French maps as *"La Riviere de la Pucelle Juine"* (the River of the Jewish Virgin) and including *"Baiouc a la Chaudepisse"* (Bayou Gonorrhea).

Like similar riverboat shantytowns that sprang up to meet the needs of randy boatmen and early traders and trappers, Bayou Sara had saloons aplenty, just as did Natchez-Under-the-Hill, where it was said that for a time the only thing cheaper than a woman's body was a man's life. King of the flatboatmen, of course, was the legendary Mike Fink, who boasted, "I can outrun, out hop, throw down, drag out and lick any man in the country. I'm a salt-river roarer, I am; I love the wimming and I'm chock full of fight."

In her book of recollections entitled *Bayou Sara: Then and Now*, Beulah Smith Watts recalls being told that Bayou Sara in its earliest days was

a notorious river town. Ladies did not dare go on the street in daytime unescorted and never after dark. Barrooms were plentiful. Max Mann and Ben Mann each had a barroom. Henry Martin, George and Ellis

Lithograph by Henry Lewis on the Mississippi River ca. 1846-48. Location noted as "Bayou Sacra" is likely Bayou Sara, with St. Francisville seen on bluff in background. Published in *Das illustrirte Mississippithal*, (1854-57). Acquired from Wikimedia Commons.

Massey, Henry Kaufman, John Levy, and John Irvine all had barrooms. Most of them had gambling tables. No wonder there were so many drunken brawls and killings. Five men were killed in one evening, three white men and two negroes including Willie and George Rucker, Bob Brannon and Clint Briggs. Two were killed in a freak shooting. Everyone carried pistols as men today carry wallets or cigarettes.

And yet, other accounts, notably from newspaperman J.W. Dorr, called Bayou Sara, in comparison to Natchez-Under-the-Hill, "a much higher class place and did not have the reputation of being a nest of thieves, with dens of sporting women and gambling halls or for being the refuge and hideout for criminals of all sorts. Like all river towns, it has 'spots,' but these were well policed and in no way interfered with the enormous amount of business carried on."

An 1888 piece in *Louisiana Churchman and Industrial News*, one of several papers published in Bayou Sara from 1838 through 1889 (the others being the *Louisiana Chronicle* and the *Ledger)*, describes Bayou Sara as having been established on the batture extending from the Mississippi River back to the line of hills upon which St. Francisville developed—its base being a deposit of the river through the ages. "The memory of no historian whose annals we have had the privilege of consulting extends back to the period when the waters of the mighty river washed the feet of these grand old hills," the article attests, "and yet they certainly did at some remote period, as the conformation of the surrounding country amply testifies."

In the glory days before the Civil War, Bayou Sara was one of the busiest ports on the Mississippi River between New Orleans and Memphis, certainly the largest between New Orleans and Natchez in 1850. A mile of brick warehouses lined the waterfront to store cotton awaiting shipment to factors in New Orleans and thence to mills and markets up East or in England. Besides early nineteenth-century flatboat traffic and cargo barges plying the Mississippi River, later fast packets and fanciful steamboats pulled up to the banks to disgorge passengers and deliveries, as sweating roustabouts piled bales so high around the sides that the boats themselves all but disappeared from view. On some days, there may have been several

A KEEL-BOAT ON THE MISSISSIPPI   302.10

First flatboats and then keelboats equipped with sails were loaded with produce and goods for markets downriver in the 1700s; the boatmen often pulled into the calmer waters of Bayou Sara creek to spend the night out of the river's swift currents. Courtesy of the West Feliciana Historical Society.

dozen big steamboats lined up along the banks.

Bayou Sara grew into an important river port, with arriving vessels laden with the produce of the entire Mississippi Valley delivering the merchandise and trade goods ordered by the stores for resale. It became a shipping point for the cotton and produce from the rich surrounding plantation country and an arrival point for the fine furnishings and other finished goods the wealthy planters imported to beautify their homes. A regular fleet of luxurious steamboats picked up or discharged Feliciana folk bound to or from New Orleans and points beyond, some traveling for pleasure and some on business. It was the easiest and most comfortable means of travel back then, although not necessarily the safest.

The first steamboat, *The New Orleans* designed by Robert Fulton, came down the Mississippi River in 1811 with three passengers, Nicholas Roosevelt, his pregnant wife, and their dog, plus crew and staff, surviving Indians, fire, the New Madrid earthquake, and the baby's birth to arrive in New Orleans. By 1816 Henry Shreve had designed *The Washington* with a shallow hull more suitable for river passage.

∽

The extensive residential sections of Bayou Sara had elaborate homes for the prosperous merchants, and the bustling commercial district boasted fine hotels and livery stables, saloons, and emporiums peddling goods shipped in from around the world. Even some of the nation's finest cabinetmakers had outlets to provide custom furnishings for the magnificent plantation houses being erected in the surrounding countryside. Bayou Sara had boarding houses, drugstores and apothecaries, saw mills and lumber yards, livestock traders and butchers, fish markets, fairgrounds, baseball fields, grocers and drygoods stores, post and express offices, clothiers, ice houses, and banks.

The first church built in Bayou Sara was the Methodist Church on Sun Street in 1844 with its upstairs gallery providing seating for slaves attending services and, occasionally, safe refuge for townsfolk during high water—though after years of flooding and a devastating fire, in 1896 the congregation rebuilt atop the bluff in St. Francisville, salvaging what lumber they could and reusing the original bell. Roman Catholics in Bayou Sara were periodically ministered to by priests from across the river and elsewhere. In 1840 Catholic services were held in the upper floor of the old market house, and after it was burned during the Civil War, in private homes or the courthouse. Early Bayou Sara Episcopalians trudged

The Methodist Church was built in Bayou Sara in 1844, with an upper gallery that pro-
vided safe refuge from the rising waters. The congregation eventually moved up the hill into
St. Francisville to escape periodic flooding by the Mississippi River. Courtesy of the West
Feliciana Historical Society.

up the hill to St. Francisville's Grace Episcopal Church where the state's second oldest congregation of that faith had come together in 1827. The Jewish population gathered in one of the Bayou Sara hotels or in Julius Freyhan's Opera House until they could build Temple Sinai in the early 1900s in St. Francisville.

∽

Bayou Sara was incorporated by act of the state legislature in 1842: "Be it enacted by the Senate and House of Representatives of the State of Louisiana that all the tract or portion of land situated in the parish of West Feliciana, on the east bank of the Mississippi River laid off and divided into squares, lots and streets, as embraced and designated in the figurative map or plan of the town of Bayou Sara, formerly called New Valentia shall continue to be designated and known as the town of Bayou Sara, and that all the white male inhabitants of said town are hereby declared to be a body corporate." In the early 1800s Ambrose Smith and his father John (a Baptist preacher, Ohio Congressman and land speculator), had ambitious plans for a village, wharves and warehouses near the mouth of Bayou Sara, but New Valencia was a failure due to title disputes with the infamous Kemper brothers as well as John Smith's questionable associations with Aaron Burr, which led to his disgrace. That charter was repealed in 1847 and a new one granted on March 14, 1850:

> Beginning on the east side of Bayou Sara at its mouth, running along said side of said Bayou to junction with Fountain Bayou, thence running along the east side of Fountain Bayou to its intersection with Salser Bayou at or near the residence of B. Bertus, including said residence and all on the south side of said Salsers Bayou until it joins a line to be run from Mississippi River, about one hundred and sixty yards below the residence of Edwin Leet, and terminating at the point designated on Salsers Bayou hereby created and made a corporation, the name and style of Bayou Sara.

Qualified voters of Bayou Sara were to elect a mayor and five councilmen on the first Monday in April each year. From the Oath Books of West Feliciana Parish the following served as mayors:

James A. Marks (1862); John P. Mumford (1868 and 1869); E.W. Whiteman (1873); H.S. Welton (1874); John F. Irvine (1874); Matthew Reilly (1875); B.T. White (1875); E.W. Whiteman (1876); L. Vresinsky (1876); John F. Irvine (1876); George Baier (1911 and 1912); J.H. Logan (1913 and 1914); and Henry Kaufman (1919-1921).

The longest term, according to the *True Democrat* of 1896, was when the office of Bayou Sara mayor was occupied by John F. Irvine for the previous fifteen years, except for an interval of two years when F.M. Mumford served.

Bayou Sara before the Civil War grew by leaps and bounds in spite of several devastating fires, one in the 1850s destroying more than fifty structures in the very heart of commerce in the town. The port city endured even more destructive shelling and torching by Union forces during the Civil War after the *Sumter*, a Yankee gunboat grounded near Bayou Sara in 1862 and abandoned by its crew as they went off to get help, was destroyed by Confederates. In retaliation, the Union ironclad *Essex*, arriving to assist the grounded boat, "opened upon the town and completely destroyed it, and then went ashore and burnt up St. Francisville a mile back from the river," according to one newspaper dispatch from New Orleans, although the reports of the demise of the two persistent little communities were somewhat premature.

∞

Bayou Sara also had, at its outskirts, the terminus for one of the country's first standard gauge railroads, the West Feliciana Railroad, chartered in 1831 as a feeder line to haul the all-important cotton crop from the highly productive plantations in southwest Mississippi and Louisiana to the bustling port. Advertisements for railroad workers promised wages from $20 to $60, with deck passage on board riverboats from Pittsburg to Bayou Sara costing from $6 to $8. One ad in a Pennsylvania newspaper cried "2,000 Men Wanted" in October 1836, with members of the railroad firm to be in Pittsburg and Cincinnati offering steady employment for laborers, carpenters, hewers, and woodchoppers, with favorable winter weather allowing year-round working conditions in the "healthy, moderate and dry" climate.

The rail line was to be laid out "on ground about four hundred feet above the highest water mark of the Mississippi River," and the ads promised "this paper is not issued for the purpose of deceiving laborers, as the subscribers have been on the ground, and have a large force already employed, and are desirous of employing a still greater one, who will be promptly paid whenever they earn it." Track was laid for twenty-seven miles, the crude rails of wood capped with thin strips of iron and construction costing $25,000 per mile. One of the provisions of the original charter was that "no trains shall be operated on the Sabbath."

A West Feliciana Railroad engine plows through the floodwaters.
Courtesy of the West Feliciana Historical Society.

Railroad tracks are seen at the water's edge of Bayou Sara.
Courtesy of the West Feliciana Historical Society.

This screeching, belching "iron horse" would eventually supersede the steamboats so that commercial traffic became reliant on the railroads and bypassed little river ports like Bayou Sara. By 1905 the Louisiana Railway and Navigation Co. had run its first locomotive into Bayou Sara with rails and ties to push towards Angola and meet the line from Shreveport. Within a few years the railway company was handling Bayou Sara mail service instead of the riverboats.

∽

But there were more immediate problems, for Bayou Sara sat right on the banks of "Ol' Man River," fed by seven thousand streams and tributaries draining more than a third of the continental United States, some 1.15 million square miles.

The river was its blessing, and the river was its curse. It enriched, fertilized, and transported. But as it gave, it also took away. The steamboats with their overheated boilers blew up midstream, flinging flaming passengers

Foot of the hill coming into Bayou Sara from St. Francisville. Above, the area is shown under floodwaters and below, the muddy aftermath left when the waters receded. Courtesy of the West Feliciana Historical Society.

The Bayou Sara post office. By 1927, when the town's charter was revoked, there was only one registered voter in Bayou Sara. Courtesy of the West Feliciana Historical Society.

into the roiling waves. And each spring the river swelled with melted snow and rain, raging torrents bursting through crevasses in the flimsy levees erected privately by individual planters and farmers, inundating surrounding areas with ten or twenty feet of water, sweeping away crops and livestock and entire communities, half-submerged houses floating down river with whole families clinging precariously to peaked roofs.

∞

By 1909, after floods and fires, yellow fever epidemics and wartime shelling, the port city of Bayou Sara had seen better days. A newspaper report of that year gives an amusing account of a scheduled visit by the battleship *Mississippi*. The chairman of the local Bayou Sara reception committee, chagrined at accounts of elaborate banquets and balls given to honor the ship's officers and crew at New Orleans and Baton Rouge, wired its captain, "This is a hell of a place to receive anybody, but we will do the best we can." And when a newspaper correspondent, tongue in cheek, wired back inquiring whether civilians should dress in high silk hats and frock coats during Bayou Sara's welcome ceremony, the response was a hospitable "Not necessary to wear anything at all. Come ahead!"

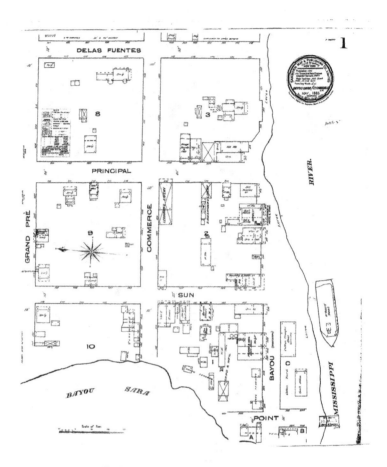

Sanborn map for Bayou Sara (1885).
Courtesy of West Feliciana Historical Museum, Kilbourne Collection.

It is revealing to contrast the Sanborn maps of Bayou Sara in 1885 and 1922. Descending the Public Road from St. Francisville into Bayou Sara, the earlier map shows numerous structures lining the major thoroughfares of Principal and Sun Streets as well as Point, De Las Eventas, and Del Oxiente Streets, crossed by Mansanta, Baton Rouge, Queen, Grand Pre, and Commerce Streets running parallel to the river. The levee is lined with cotton yards and sheds; a wharf boat is shown on the water. These squares are nearly empty on the 1922 map.

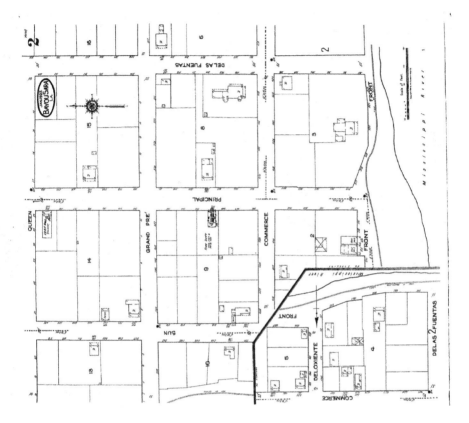

Sanborn map for Bayou Sara (1922) showing the impact of near-yearly flooding; many of the structures that once crowded the streets were either washed away or moved up the hill into St. Francisville. Courtesy of West Feliciana Historical Museum, Kilbourne Collection.

In 1926 the charter of Bayou Sara was revoked and soon its post office was closed as well. In 1927 the river flooded 26,000 square miles and left over 600,000 people homeless and huddled in Red Cross tent cities along the Lower Mississippi, the most extensive flood in the history of the country and the incentive to implement serious coordinated levee control. Bayou Sara was essentially obliterated, with only a few of its sturdier structures hauled up the hill to St. Francisville on the bluff behind teams of straining oxen.

2

The Founder of Bayou Sara

Occupied first by the peaceful Houma Indians, who were driven out by the fierce Tunica tribe, the Bayou Sara/St. Francisville area is rich in Indian artifacts bespeaking a thriving trade with European adventurers traversing the Mississippi River and exploring its shores as early as the 1600s. The French established the first formal settlement around 1729 near a small fort, Ste. Reyne aux Tonicas, which was soon abandoned. When France lost the rest of Louisiana to Spain, her vast territory east of the Mississippi, including West Feliciana, went to England in 1763 and became known as West Florida.

In the 1770s settlement began in earnest around a monastery and cemetery established by Capuchin monks from across the river, who crossed over the waters to bury their dead high on the St. Francisville bluffs safe from flooding. For the rest of the century the area was dominated by England and later Spain. In 1780 the governor of Spanish Louisiana, Bernardo de Galvez, ousted the British from that portion of West Florida he called Feliciana.

In the last years of the eighteenth century, the king of Spain issued large land grants to Eastern Seaboard adventurers in an effort to stabilize the Florida colonies. This led to an influx of primarily Anglo-Saxon settlers into early Feliciana, attracted by the rich fertile soil, plentiful water supply, and long growing seasons. It would be these English planters who established the large plantations cultivating immense acreages of cash crops—first indigo and then cotton and sugarcane. Stretched along the Great River Road, from New Orleans to Natchez, the planters of cotton and cane comprised more than two-thirds of America's known millionaires in the mid-1800s; it was no wonder that this lower stretch of the Mississippi River came to be known as the River of Riches.

The tax rolls of 1853 show that the entire parish of West Feliciana, including Bayou Sara and St. Francisville, contained 2,231 free whites, 70 free blacks, and 10,298 slaves, who produced in that year: 2,873 hogsheads of sugar; 4,318 barrels of molasses; 334,000 bushels of corn; and 23,860 bales of cotton selling at about $70 a bale. Some of the plantations in the surrounding countryside covered thousands of acres and had hundreds of slaves, many of them skilled artisans, blacksmiths and builders, tanners and wheelwrights, furniture makers, gardeners, seamstresses, spinners and weavers.

But not everybody lived on a plantation or owned the enormous acreages required for agricultural success. Along the Mississippi River corridor in the little port cities and towns that were the centers of commerce and the supply sources for the outlying plantations, merchants and small business owners set up housekeeping, dependent upon the planters who purchased goods and services but without the burdens and responsibilities of owning land or maintaining extensive work forces to cultivate cash crops.

∞

In the late 1700s, a Scotsman by way of Virginia named John Mills arrived from Natchez to found a cotton port and trading post right on the Mississippi River where Bayou Sara emptied its waters. Mills arrived with his brother Gilbert in the Felicianas sometime prior to 1781 when the Catholic Church across the river from Bayou Sara recorded John's marriage to Perine Marionneau, according to research compiled by Virginia Lobdell Jennings. He had operated a sawmill in Natchez, Mississippi, in partnership with an Englishman from Liverpool named Isaac Johnson. When the mill was lost to high water, both Mills and Johnson moved south—Johnson to establish Troy Plantation just below St. Francisville and Mills to purchase land at the mouth of Bayou Sara from William Wickoff in January of 1789.

Content to establish his trading post on low land near the river commerce, John Mills sought higher ground for his residence after his friend John Hunter Johnson (son of Isaac) laid out the town of St. Francisville on a narrow, undulating loessial finger ridge overlooking Bayou Sara and the river. In May 1809 Mills purchased, for nine hundred pesos, four and a half building lots and commenced building the sturdy brick home that in later years would be called Propinquity. The original inventory of the building contractor included nearly 200,000 bricks, eight bushels of hair for the plaster, and a fanlight window for the attic. After Mills's death, his widow advertised the sale of "a brick house in an airy part of town," and the house was rented for some months to Judge William Center Wade, parish judge for the Feliciana district, who eventually purchased it in 1816 for $3,900.

By 1822 Propinquity had been acquired by German-born Dietrich Holl, who operated a store there and took as his assistant his handsome young nephew, Maximillian Nuebling.

John Mills farmed extensively on lands along Alexander Creek that would eventually become Rosedown Plantation. After Mills's death in 1812, part of his Spanish land grant was purchased by William Barrow, whose daughter Martha and her planter-husband Daniel Turnbull acquired the property from other heirs for $60,000 in 1829 and built the stately double-galleried Rosedown house (now a state historic site and national historic landmark).

Ironically, in the fall of 1810 both John Mills and William Barrow were two of the four well-respected and influential men chosen as representatives of the Feliciana district when the Anglo planters who had settled the Felicianas tired of Spanish rule and revolted. The Spanish had continued to claim the lands east of the Mississippi River even after the Louisiana Purchase of 1803, when Thomas Jefferson acquired, at a bargain price of $15,000,000 or four cents an acre, the entire central third of the country (including New Orleans), essentially doubling the size of the fledgling United States. The planters of these Florida Parishes got together (one of the early secret organizational meetings was held at Isaac Johnson's Troy Plantation), threw out the Spanish, and set up a revolutionary republic—a well-conceived one with a constitution similar to the United States constitution and with legislative and judicial chambers in St. Francisville, the capital of the Republic of West Florida. The Bayou Sara Horse, two companies of recruits under the leadership of Capt. Jedediah Smith and Capt. Llewellyn Griffith (separately called the Mounted Rangers or Volunteer Company of Mounted Riflemen and the Troop of Horse), played an important role in the revolution. The republic lasted a grand total of seventy-four days before the group joined the rest of Louisiana, which eventually became a state in 1812.

An earlier rebellion, an abortive one in 1804, had gained less than universal support among the planters; its organizers, the rough and rowdy Kemper brothers, were seen as true patriots by some and as renegade outlaws by others. Bayou Sara's founder John Mills wrote of being accosted by one of the brothers, "a rifle gun and long knife sticking at his breast, a pistol sticking in the waistband of his breeches, and a dagger hanging at his side." Another who crossed the Kempers reportedly had his ears cut off "with a dull knife" and displayed, pickled in wine, at the family tavern just across the Mississippi state line.

In a letter written in 1807 to a New York cousin, now preserved in the LSU archives, John Mills described the virtues of Bayou Sara's location:

> It is fortunate for us that we can get supplies from the upper country. Those that have money need not want—you would be astonished, I am sure, if you could spend one week at the Mouth of Bayou Sara at this season of the year (altho [sic] you live in a commercial city) to see the best quantity of produce that passes daily to New Orleans, which promises to be one of the great commercial cities of the world—the increase of population consequently of produce in the upper country is wonderful. Boats have been descending ever since the breaking up of the Ice, which begins in the more southerly regions first. And as the Rivers break up more northwardly, the Boats come on loaded with every kind of produce that the upper empire affords or that ingenuity can invent. Flour, corn meal, whiskey and Cider, Pork and Beef, live state fed Beaver, Venison and Mutton Hams, great quantities of bacon, Horses in great numbers, which fetches high prices owing to the superior strength and figure— great quantities of butter, Lard, soap & Candles, and everything else that the country affords or that is wanted here. Many of us depends on this market for supplies particularly for such articles as we can buy cheaper than we can make, you must know we are great calculators—that when the same labour that will make a Barrel of Irish Potatoes in this country, can be disposed of in making Cotton as to pay for 2 Barrels brought to our door from above. We prefer buying of these and so with everything else, our country produces all these things with less labour than the upper country, but Cotton & Sugar is the most profitable, articles they cannot make. High up the different River Cumberland makes some cotton of an inferior quality.

He also discusses the vagaries of the weather and its impact on all of life in this agricultural region.

> In my last, I mentioned to you that I was fearful we should suffer much for the want of Indian Corn, or rather that we already were suffering but that we had plentiful supplies of flour, etc. This may seem a paradox to you, who are not in the habit of using that kind of grain much. You must know, that Corn in this country is truly the staff of life. More than two-thirds of the bread eaten in this country by the whites is made of that grain, it is almost the whole food of Thousands of Negroes, the facility in raising of it is such in this country the lands new and fresh, that there is perhaps a greater consumption of that necessary grain made here than in any other place on the Globe, in proportion to the number of people. Horses are fed all the year without measure, and that in great numbers,

working Oxen, Hogs and poultry destroy great quantities, and what adds much to the general demand is the great numbers of Choctaw and other Indians, who is always amongst us, wandering from place to place, with their families. The want of Corn is such at this time that the poor creatures has all left us, and I suppose taken to the woods, to get something to eat. They kill our Cattle and Hogs rather than starve. People that can command cash may supply themselves with any quantity of Flour at the most reasonable rate. The best Superfine sells now at our landing at 6 piastres the Barrel, but flour won't answer to feed our working creatures, without which our next crop will likewise fail, and I assure you there is an alarming prospect as yet owing to the want of food for working creatures, and a great drought that now prevails, and no appearance of rain. So that seed lies in the ground and cannot come up, and what is up is dwindling to nothing, yet the advantages of the climate and soil is such that if the season soon comes favourable we shall no doubt make plenty—we are particularly unfortunate with our Cotton Crop. A cut worm has been very troublesome. We have been obliged to plant already 2 and 3 times, the last planting cannot come up, owing to the want of moisture.

Nor was the temperature much help to struggling area farmers. In a region not known for snow or severe winter weather, Mills expressed surprise at the lack of snow or rain in New York, having expected because of his own area's frigid winter

that you would all be frozen to Death. . . . Such a winter was never known or heard of here, as the cold set in early and lasted without interruption until very late. Constant fronts, we had a snow near 6 inches deep, which lay on the ground for several days before it entirely disappeared—our stock, cattle and horse, Sheep and Hogs suffered much. Many died, and but little labour could be done by our almost naked Negroes the whole winter.

3

Immigration

A preserved collection of letters from Max Nuebling, covering the period from October 1822 (as he leaves his home in Germany to join his uncle in Louisiana) to August 1826, gives in fascinating detail an intimate look at life in early Bayou Sara/St. Francisville. Young Nuebling's writings also shed light on the appeal of this fledgling new country, with all its promised opportunities and freedoms, to immigrants from the Old Country, making them willing to risk life and limb on ocean voyages that were fraught with dangers and must have seemed interminable.

Some of these immigrants, particularly those of the Jewish faith, were fleeing religious persecution in Germany, and they arrived penniless. Many of them followed the westward movement of the cotton empire, often starting their new lives as peddlers with packs on their backs, taking small housewares and necessities to isolated farm families in the days before rural delivery. Once they prospered sufficiently, they purchased a small wheeled push cart and maybe even a horse to pull it so that they could enlarge their inventories; then, perhaps later, began clerking in one of the dry-goods emporiums until they could save enough to invest in inventories for their own mercantiles. Only rarely did they invest in land; these were not planters. The Jewish immigrants brought with them skills in merchandising and financing that were sorely lacking in what was essentially an agrarian society based precariously on credit, with planters of necessity borrowing against next year's crop when that year's cash crop failed due to freezes, floods, or other uncontrollable events.

There were fortunes to be made in the thriving settlement of Bayou Sara, many of them made by the Jewish merchants who were smart enough to see the potential as the cotton empire expanded westward from depleted East Coast lands through the rich Mississippi Delta. All along the Mississippi River Valley there were close-knit Jewish communities thriving from the mid-nineteenth century, from Vicksburg to Port Gibson, Natchez to Woodville, Mississippi, and on downriver to Bayou Sara and St. Francisville and below.

Jewish tradesmen operated many of the dry goods stores and other businesses supporting the plantation empire, providing credit when needed, building cotton gins and presses, and dabbling in real estate (although as a general rule they preferred more mobile assets).When they took crops as payment, they found themselves in the cotton business as much as any planter. After the Civil War, when the banks failed, they could get credit to help their friends and neighbors get back on their feet, and as they prospered, they engaged in philanthropies, such as funding the area's first public school.

In the early years, those immigrants who were Gentiles, many from Germany like the Jewish immigrants, came seeking new lives as well—freedom from conscription or indenture and enhanced possibilities for advancement. Both groups encouraged other family members to join them in this new land of equal opportunity. This phenomenon was called chain migration, where newcomers joined established settlers. That was the situation for young Maximillian Nuebling.

At least a third of his preserved correspondence with his family back home covers his arduous trip from Germany via sailing vessel, at the mercy of pirates and frightening or frustrating weather—howling winds roiling the waves and dangerously rocking the boat, or no winds at all that left the ship becalmed for days. At six in the morning on October 4, 1822, he left Bremen and boarded the *S.S. Fortuna*, which had to sail back and forth along the River Weser, awaiting a favorable wind to reach the sea. When the ship finally entered the North Sea, Nuebling writes:

> As long as I live, I shall never forget the night from the 19th to the 20th. On this night the ship went through an awful storm. To keep from getting seasick, I remained on deck as long as possible. The waves came at the ship as high as a house, and all of us got thoroughly wet. The ship rolled so awfully that I had trouble not to be thrown out of my bunk, and I had to hold on something with both of my hands to keep from falling out. Naturally sleep was out of the question with all the noise and the rolling of the ship. I find it impossible to describe this storm, one must live through it, to know what a storm at sea really is. About 6 o'clock the following morning the storm lightened up a little, but the sea rolled so badly that I did not leave my bunk from the 20th to the 24th, but somehow I survived.

In frustration he wrote that he had been "31 days aboard this vessel, and we have not even passed the British Channel," due to storms even worse than the one in the North Sea, waves washing over the ship, railings destroyed, and several sailors feared lost overboard. Loss of barrels of

Ox team hauling log along St. Francisville's Royal Street just across from Propinquity, per-haps on the way to Bayou Sara's lumber mill that turned out some 75,000 feet of lumber daily by 1912. Courtesy of the West Feliciana Historical Society.

drinking water meant rationing, and after several terrific winter storms, he said the boat looked as if it had gone through a battle in war times. On one return to the coast of England, word came of a British ship turned over by the last storm, with loss of the entire crew except one mate and a ship's boy.

Three times the vessel turned around because of issues with winds and weather, only to start again when the breezes turned favorable, and Nuebling was reminded that winter "is always colder at sea than it is on land. . . . It is almost too much to bear. I am practically wearing all of my clothes at night to keep warm. I am wearing my shirt, underwear, stockings and 2 shawls, and cover myself with a woolen blanket and my overcoat, but somehow I cannot get warm, which is not so very strange, as my bunk is always wet from the water that comes into the cabin."

When the sea was calm enough that he didn't have to hold onto some-thing as the ship rolled, Nuebling spent his time drawing, writing letters to his family back home, and studying English from books. On one such day, he almost lost his dog to the waves.

"I wanted to give him a bath, and tied a piece of rope to his collar and threw him overboard for a swim, but when I wanted to pull him on board again, his collar slipped off and I thought I had lost him, when a sailor ran aft and, on reaching overboard, grabbed him by the ears and pulled him back aboard." This is the same dear little dog he would later have to shoot after it was bitten by a rabid animal.

Despite having departed his home on October 4, it was not until No-vember 8 that young Nuebling felt he had truly left. He wrote to his parents, "At last we have left the channel behind us. Early this morning, the wind became more favorable, and we made good time, and for the past hour, England is out of our sight. Farewell to the old world. With God's help, I hope to return to you in a few years, with my pockets full of money, from the New World, never to leave you again."

Christmas was marked aboard ship by haircuts for everyone, New Year's celebrated by toasts with a glass of beer and the enjoyment of warmer weather from the Caribbean as the vessel approached the West Indies and then the Gulf of Mexico. "We are now in the month of January, and it is warmer now than at home in midsummer." During pleasant weather, young Nuebling enjoyed the diversions of watching seabirds, flying fish, dolphins, and sharks; his curiosity regarding these unfamiliar species was insatiable, and when a dolphin was caught and prepared for dinner, the young traveler inspected the contents of its stomach and found, to his amazement, nine flying fish with three "almost alive yet."

On January 31, after fifteen weeks at sea, Nuebling noted that when the wind was low the vessel barely made eighteen miles a day, but with favorable winds could travel fifty-six miles per day. "When I left home," he wrote, "I was under the impression that I would arrive at my destination within a few days. It certainly takes patience to make a trip like this one, that seems to have no ending, and I am getting tired to see nothing but water." He would later write to friends in Germany, "I can assure you that it was an awful trip. One storm after another, and for days not a stitch of dry clothes on your body is no fun. It took 120 days to cross the ocean. All we had to drink was brandy, and the awful ship's beer."

But at last the ship reached the mouth of the Mississippi, and, after interminable delays caused by unfavorable winds, the impatient Nuebling finally left the boat and walked along shore to reach New Orleans on February 21, 1823. He then took a steamboat to Bayou Sara, leaving his baggage to catch up with him later. He wrote that the trip up the river, lined with many plantations, was a nice end to such a long and tiresome journey, "but I shall be glad when it is all over, and I do not believe that I shall ever make such a trip again." In subsequent correspondence he explains that the trip from Bremen to New Orleans was about 7,200 miles or 2,600 hours, from the mouth of the Mississippi River to New Orleans 170 miles, and from New Orleans to Bayou Sara about 150 miles.

His German uncle Dieter Holl welcomed him warmly. After a short period of illness, "no doubt due to the change in the diet," he wrote a detailed summary of his daily life.

I imagine I can hear my mother say that she wants to know how I pass every minute of my time, and will try my best to please her. Well, here goes: I arise every morning with the sun, and open the store, and take my rag, and wipe and clean every item in the store. At 8 o'clock. . . . I go to our neighbor Oldenburg to get breakfast, then back to the store, where I am a salesman, but also have many other duties to perform, such as weighing coffee, sugar, starch, cleaning bottles and filling them with wine. At 1 o'clock we eat our dinner, and I want to tell mother that it is really good and plentiful, the same as she would get in a first class hotel. The afternoon is a repetition of my morning work, and in the evening I usually go horseback riding. Dieter usually furnishes the horse, and has never yet disappointed me in loaning the horse to me. Sometimes I eat supper with Dieter. On Sundays I usually make some drawings, go horseback riding, and get my noonday meal at Dieter's. After dinner we go bowling in Dieter's garden, and in the evening I ride horseback again, or go hunting; that's how I pass my time during the day. I am not perfect in English yet, but understand enough to be able to sell anything in the store."

He had to ride horseback into the surrounding countryside to collect debts owed to his uncle's business, and he also spent a great deal of time collecting specimens of oddities to send to the folks back home, including alligator hides, snake skins, lizards, bird eggs, bird wings, a whip, dried citrus, an Indian bow and arrows, and other curiosities.

He couldn't help, he wrote, being homesick for his family and friends, and especially for the sweetheart he left behind, who seemed not to have corresponded with him once he left Germany. "The uncertainty of my dearest Lisette often takes all the courage out of me. I most certainly had ample time to think about this, and I can assure you that I have never regretted to become acquainted with this splendid girl, and I am eagerly looking forward to time when I can call her my very own, my dearly beloved wife. I have had ample opportunity to get acquainted with girls here, but God knows, I don't want no American girl for a wife." He would soon change his mind; when his elderly uncle married the lovely young ward of Mrs. Robert Percy, at whose Beech Woods plantation both artist John James Audubon and his wife Lucy were employed periodically as tutors in the 1820s. Nuebling found her fetching, and when Uncle Dieter died, he took over not only his uncle's business but also his widow, whom he wed.

Nuebling's uncle Dieter (Dietrich) Holl had the well-deserved reputation of being an honest businessman with unlimited credit, and he felt comfortable leaving his nephew in charge of his store when he travelled.

Nuebling writes, "Uncle Dieter is contemplating a trip to New Orleans, and from there by boat to New York, Philadelphia and Baltimore and Washington City, to buy merchandise for our store. From there he will return to New Orleans by riverboat via the Mississippi. He can purchase the merchandise up North for about one-half of the price he would have to pay in New Orleans, and he will make a good profit on them."

Often in his correspondence the young immigrant attempted to explain to his parents in Germany the appeal of his new community and country, expressing pride at his salary of $400 a year, "the equivalent of 1,000 *guldun* over there, and nothing to be laughed at." And he constantly encouraged his brothers to join him if their uncle should offer a position, no matter what salary he might offer, for the cost of living was low, no more than $100 to $150 a year, and the free and equitable lifestyle a vast improvement over that in the Old Country.

> Good Lord, what a difference between the free and easy life here, and over there. Overbearing people that look down upon everyone else, because they hold some kind of official position and think they are better than everyone else, are unknown here. . . . A man here is valued here according to what he is, and what he can do, and not the position he holds. Our sheriff, who holds a high position here, is the most friendly man one can meet; he talks to everyone, and any man can talk to him. Liberty is the greatest gift of manhood, and here we have real liberty, and I have no intention ever to return to my old home and end my days as a slave. Of course, I want to see you again, but only on a visit, and then to return to the Free America.

Conscription was a worry. Nuebling's family wrote to him that conscription was to be enforced that coming year, and he would be fined 500 marks if not present. "That is news to me," he responds,

> and I had never thought about it. I have no money, and still owe to my uncle a considerable sum of money, and am unable to pay this fine, but I think I know a way out of it. The constitution of Wurtemberg permits its citizens to emigrate to any country they choose to. Do you think you could get such permission for me? If you could, I would be free of conscription. I would lose my citizenship, but would rather lose that, than pay this sum of money. I like this country much better, and should I ever make a trip back home, I could always buy my citizenship back again."

Coping with river floods, heat, and illness were all part of life in early Bayou Sara.

We expect to have a difficult summer here this year, as the river has overflown the levees, causing the entire neighborhood to be under water, and when the water is going back into the river, it will leave nothing but swamps, and cause a lot of illness. The temperature is very high and will go still higher in August, as I have been told, but thank God I am still in good health, and took a laxative last week, and expect to go through this summer without any too great trouble, by eating and drinking moderately.

When the backyard smokehouse, where some six thousand pounds of pork was being smoked to sell in the store, caught fire during his uncle's absence, Nuebling cried "Fire" and the neighbors all came running, "but as we had to carry the water in buckets from the Mississippi River, as there are no fire apparatus in town, it was useless, and the whole building with its contents went up in smoke, and we had our hands full in saving the buildings in the immediate neighborhood." Overheated and exhausted by his frantic attempts to extinguish the fire, he was stricken with high fever and delirium. He was unsuccessfully treated by the local doctor for days until his Uncle Dieter "tried one of his own cures, by giving me 2 doses of opium, and the fever disappeared immediately. The doctor, who came later, told me that that was a dose for a horse, but not for a human being, but that is because he does not know what a German is able to assimilate."

In response to questions from his family, Nuebling sprinkles his replies with statistics and explanations of cultural differences.

The Mississippi here is 7/8 and in New Orleans 3/4 miles wide. We have now low water, but still a steamboat with 1,400 bales of cotton, each of 400 lbs., can go with safety up and down the river, without touching bottom. In high water, the river is about 30 feet deeper. New Orleans has a police force of about 50 men. We have to pay $50 annual tax to operate our business. For carriage hire we pay $2, and we pay $1 as wage for negroes. A young man like myself has to work 12 days on street repair, and if he cannot work, he must pay $6 as a penalty. Dieter, who has lived longer than I in this country and knows more about it than I do, told me to tell you that the laws here are very simple, that everyone can understand them, and that all laws are enforced more justly than in any country he knows of, and that the judges and governors of each state are elected by the people themselves, and that everyone can get justice in court, no matter who he is.

After two years living and working in the Bayou Sara/St. Francisville area, Max Nuebling exhibited a pronounced patriotism and love for his adopted country as he wrote to his family members in Germany:

> Your kings are not satisfied, unless they can destroy some other country, and even try to go to some other hemisphere to create a lot of trouble, and even try to come over here. But just let them come and try it, and we'll give them the same that we gave the Englishmen. They seem to forget that there is a great, wide ocean between them and this country. Those people don't know anything of this great free country that is controlled by the patriotism of its free people. I feel sorry for any country that would try to conquer this free America. We would send them back where they came from, and but few would see their own homeland again. European war methods are useless here, and even if they should send 100,000 troops over here, it would do no good. The American does not remain in the open, to be shot down by some enemy commanded by perhaps a fifteen-year-old officer; no, the Americans go into the wilderness and shoot from behind trees where no one can see them, and they are all very good sharpshooters and never miss at anything they aim. I hope to God that our own people will not come over here under such conditions.

In the four-year period covered by the collected letters of Max Nuebling preserved by the West Feliciana Historical Society, courtesy of the owners of Propinquity, he witnessed many changes as both Bayou Sara, on the banks of the Mississippi, and its sister city St. Francisville, on the bluffs overlooking it, grew and developed. Writing that St. Francisville had doubled in size since his uncle Dieter had first arrived, he describes their house as "a very large stone house and several smaller ones," while most of the structures in town were built of wood. This house today is known as Propinquity, built in 1809 of 200,000 bricks, one of the earliest structures on historic Royal Street. According to historian Elisabeth K. Dart, the artist Audubon and his wife shopped for supplies here in the 1820s—a reasonable assertion since both the artist and his wife would have been acquainted with the young woman who married first Dieter Holl and then, upon his death, his nephew Max Nuebling.

In St. Francisville, Nuebling boasted that there were two schools and a small church, with outlying plantations composed of large acreages used mostly to raise sugarcane, with slaves living in small houses near the main structures. The smaller farmers planted Turkish wheat and lots of corn as fodder for cattle and horses. "Most of our victuals," he writes, "such as smoked and salted meat, flower [*sic*] and various fruits is shipped by riverboat, and comes mostly from Kentucky and Ohio." He was proud that his uncle had formed a new partnership with Mr. John H. Mills, founder of Bayou Sara, the firm name being D. Holl & Co., and especially pleased to have been hired for three years as bookkeeper at $600 the first year, $800 the second, and $1,000 the third; "much more than I could ever expect to earn in Germany."

In the summer of 1825, Nuebling wrote to his uncle, then on a trip back to Germany, that the business was doing well, with sales in the store of $30,191.03 from January to June, and credit accounts of $24,990.45 to June. Dry goods merchandise shipped downriver by Uncle Dieter finally arrived by the end of September after steamboat delays, and partner Mills "thought at first that the amount of the merchandise would be more than we could dispose in our business, but changed his mind after we had sold over $8,000 worth this month already." Riding about the countryside to collect payments due the business, young Nuebling wrote to his travelling uncle, "I do not know at this time how the collections will turn out, but hope they will be satisfactory. I often wish you were home again. You may rest assured that I shall at all times do the best I can, and I have always considered myself to be the best collector, after you, as you have been my teacher and have showed me the art to collect money due without making enemies."

In 1825 he described to envious contemporaries back in Germany

how I pass the time of the day. At daybreak, the old negress knocks on my door and calls me. I open the door and let her come in to make a fire in the fireplace, while I crawl back in bed until the room is good and warm, when I really get up, sit in front of the fireplace and smoke a cigar. With sunrise the old negress and a younger one are coming back again and ask for a drink. I get my bottle of French cognac and fill a glass, and after taking a good drink myself, give the balance to the 2 negresses. Then I go down to the store, take a broom, and sweep the entire store out. At 8 o'clock a small negro brings my shoes, shining like a looking glass, also my coat, and I go to breakfast, consisting of coffee, ham, beefsteak, pancakes and bread and butter. After breakfast I remain in the store as a salesman until dinner time. At 4 o'clock my day usually is finished, when I get my horse, and go riding or hunting. At night, we drink tea in winter and lemonade in summertime, and eat smoked herrings, oysters, cheese and bread and butter for supper. After supper I usually visit one of my friends to pass the time away. On Sundays, I usually go hunting, or take my canoe and pull it down the bayou.

Yellow fever was a constant threat. Nuebling recorded how he took various medicines to ward off yellow fever and avoid doctor bills, almost killing himself one time by mistake.

My medicine against the fever, at one time consisted of 58 grams of calomel that I took within 4 days, and at another time I took 2 drops of arsenic, 3 times per day for 8 days, but these cures are effective. Last summer I almost made a fatal mistake. I had another touch of the fever, and sat in the store shivering. As some planters were in the store buying supplies, I could not leave the store, but finally I felt so miserable that I had to send them away, and I went into my room to get myself a drink of spirits, but by mistake I got the wrong bottle that contained laudanum and took a drink out of it. Within half an hour I became delirious, and made such a noise that our negro, that had been working in the garden, came into the house to find out what the trouble seemed to be, and at once called a doctor, who pumped out the contents of my stomach and brought me back to normalcy. He most certainly saved my life.

In a letter to his parents dated June 10, 1826, he reported that his uncle had been married on May 11, Nuebling's birthday,

and I am very fond of my new aunt. She is really very nice, and the both of them are very happy. Our little home looks like a real home now, and we often spend the evenings together, amusing ourselfs [sic]. I don't know what to do about my former love affair with Lissette. I have not heard from her for the past two years, and I am afraid that she has married someone else, which probably is the best way out and secures her a home for the future, and not the uncertainty of waiting for me and perhaps becoming an old maid. I wish her all the happiness she so richly deserves. Since my uncle married, he is determined to establish his home in America and to remain here the balance of his days, and I most probably will do the same. But still, it is my wish that father would make inquiries and let me know what she is doing." Later he writes, "I can now also tell you that my aunt has hopes of becoming a mother to the joy of uncle. She is such a nice woman, and if I could find one like her, I would not hesitate to get married without delay.

There are no later references to the dear Lisette back in Germany.

When the marriage late in life to a much younger bride proved too taxing for Uncle Dieter Holl, who did not live to see his first wedding anniversary, his handsome young nephew stepped ably into the breach, taking responsibility for both his uncle's store and widow, whom he soon wed.

The widow Holl's relationship with both John James Audubon and his wife Lucy led to a deep friendship between the Audubons and Nuebling. Audubon found the young man "well-educated and sensible of the arts," and Lucy frequently patronized the store in the 1820s, her main purchases being paint and paper for her pupils and sewing supplies for herself.

4

The Merchants

In 1860, a New Orleans newspaperman named J.W. Dorr wrote of Bayou Sara:

If St. Francisville is stronger on the ornamental, Bayou Sara is out of sight ahead of her on the practical, for she does all the business and a great deal of business is done, too. It is a thriving and bustling place, and contains some of the most extensive and heavily stocked stores in Louisiana, outside of New Orleans and there are few in New Orleans even which can surpass in value of stock, the concern of Meyers, Hoffman and Co., dry goods dealers and direct importers. The principal merchants of the place are Whiteman Bros., F.V. Leake & Co., Hatch & Irvine, and Parr and Winter—receiving, forwarding and general commission merchants and dealers in groceries and western produce. C.E. Toorsen and A. Levy & Co., dry goods and general merchandise, R. Barton, books, stationery and periodic depot. There are also a variety of smaller but apparently prosperous establishments, restaurants, bar-rooms, etc., and all the other aspects of a small city. A prominent object in the town, occupying a very handsome building is Robinson Mumford's Bank of Exchange, W.T. Mumford teller. China Grove Hotel is the principal house of entertainment, there being, besides smaller establishments, a very large and comfortably arranged wharfboat which, however, is not doing a very prosperous business, the majority of citizens being opposed to its location there. There is a Methodist Church in Bayou Sara, Rev. Thomas Donner, pastor.

Among the other prominent business interests of Bayou Sara is horse dealing, it being the great horse market for the surrounding country. Large droves of horses are brought here for sale from Kentucky and elsewhere. Messrs. Henshaw and Haile have very extensive stables and do a great deal in horse flesh. Bayou Sara is the river terminus of the West Feliciana Railroad. The depot stands upon the levee in the lower part of the town, having been moved from the upper part above Bayou Sara, a troublesome and unnavigable estuary which could not be permanently bridged, save at great cost. Bayou Sara has a post office. There is one paper published in the parish, *The Bayou Sara Ledger*, an able and well

known journal, edited and conducted by Jas. R. Marks who is mayor of
the town of Bayou Sara.

Many of the early Bayou Sara merchants were Jewish. In 1820 there
were only 2,700 Jews in the entire United States, but through the mid-
1800s waves of immigrants arrived to escape anti-Semitism, particularly
from Bavaria and the German states along the Rhine and Alsace-Lorraine
in pre-industrial France. Forbidden to own land in the Old Country, these
immigrants found their expertise in merchandising and finance filled a
crucial gap in an agrarian society like the Cotton Kingdom, as they followed the westward movement of the cotton empire from depleted eastern
fields to the rich fertile lands of the Mississippi River corridor.

The whole southern economy in the Cotton Kingdom was balanced
precariously on credit extensions at every level, and the rural merchants
played an important role in this agrarian system, providing the dry goods
and farming equipment, with the shrewd business sense to survive the ebb
and flow of a fluctuating economy based on risky crops and credit. After
the Civil War, the Jewish merchants were able to extend life-saving credit
to suffering planters and sharecroppers, and when the large cotton factor-
age firms failed to recover after the war, the country storekeepers became
pivotal figures in cotton marketing and financing. At a time when cash
was in short supply and banks unreliable, their stores had the family and
business contacts to provide far-reaching credit arrangements that allowed
them to become conduits for funneling much-needed cash into rural areas.

As these hard-working immigrants prospered, the South became the
center of the Jewish population in the country, offering religious and political freedom, as well as the possibility of social and financial success.
From Vicksburg to Port Gibson, from Natchez to Woodville, from Bayou
Sara and St. Francisville to New Orleans, there were thriving Jewish communities; Donaldsonville had more Jewish mayors than any other southern
town, and even the Confederacy had outstanding Jewish officials like Sec-
retary of State Judah P. Benjamin. In the St. Francisville/Bayou Sara area,
important names included:

- Max Dampf, born in Germany's Black Forest, who served on
  the bank board, was a member of the Board of Supervisors of
  Election, had a general merchandise store, and was called "a
  wide-awake progressive businessman and valued member of
  society";
- Joseph Stern, who arrived at age nineteen in 1867 from Weis-

baden to operate a livery and horse and mule market;

- L. Bach, whose company sold goods wholesale and retail;
- Moritz Rosenthal, a shoemaker who arrived in a wagon pulled by oxen and whose son dealt in imported dry goods. (It would be his granddaughter Hannah who saw to it that the Hebrew Rest cemetery was kept in immaculate condition all the days of her life.);
- Abe Stern, who traded horses and mules;
- Joseph Goldman, who had a bar room and grocery store;
- M.C. Levy, who handled general merchandise;
- Adolph Teutsch, who came from Bavaria and also handled general merchandise;
- Picard and Weil, who sold plantation supplies;
- Morris Burgas, who kept books and managed cotton warehouses and a mercantile house for his uncle;
- Max Mann, who owned a saloon in Bayou Sara, housed in a typical raised two-story, double-galleried wooden building

Joseph Stern came to this country at age nineteen in 1867 and operated a thriving livery business and horse and mule market in Bayou Sara in the days before automobiles. Courtesy of the Thomas H. and Joan W. Gandy Photograph Collection, acquired from the West Feliciana Historical Society.

Max Mann's, in a double-galleried two-story wooden building with fancy upper gallery rail, was one of many saloons in Bayou Sara, selling tobacco, cigars, ice-cold Schlitz beer for 15 cents a bottle, and crockery jugs of Five Feathers Whiskey. Courtesy of the Thomas H. and Joan W. Gandy Photograph Collection, Louisiana and Lower Mississippi Valley Collections, LSU Libraries, Baton Rouge, La.

with a fancy gallery rail above. He sold tobacco, cigars, genuine Schlitz ice-cold beer for 15 cents a bottle, and was the sole agent for Five Feathers Whiskey. After a disastrous flood in 1893, Max Mann moved his saloon to Ferdinand Street in upper St. Francisville and built a nice house for himself on Royal Street.

Accepted as contributing members of their adopted communities along the Mississippi River corridor, these immigrants, as they succeeded in business, supported public works and served in important civic offices. Synagogues and temples were built, cemeteries established, and charitable organizations formed as the Jews shared their prosperity in great philanthropies.

cx/o

Typical was Julius Freyhan, who arrived penniless in America at age twenty-one in 1851, took the oath of allegiance to become a U.S. citizen, and by the time he died in 1904 was described as one of the wealthiest

Saloon patron sitting atop sandbagged mudboxes used to keep floodwaters out of structures; Silver Feathers Whiskey sign advertises house specialty. Courtesy of the West Feliciana Historical Society.

and most respected men in the state. When the Civil War started, Freyhan joined his friends and neighbors in the conflict—although he served as a non-combatant musician in the Fourth Louisiana Infantry, Company D, West Feliciana Rifles. He served until 1863 when, perhaps tiring of a war in which he had little stake, he deserted, was captured, and ended up imprisoned for the duration of the war.

Once back in Bayou Sara, he built up a business empire that spilled over into St. Francisville and consisted of stores, saloons, cotton gins, gristmills, a sawmill, and a dry goods mercantile selling everything from buggies to coffins. J. Freyhan and Company, later known as M. & E. Wolf when his brothers-in-law Morris and Emanuel Wolf took over the business, served as the principle source of supplies for a dozen Louisiana parishes and southwest Mississippi counties, in a year selling one-million-dollars worth of goods and handling fourteen thousand bales of cotton. Store billheads from Freyhan's emporiums in both Bayou Sara and, later, St. Francisville advertised: plows, cultivators, barb fence wire, dry goods, clothing, hats, gents' furnishing goods, boots, shoes, western produce, general merchandise, buggies, furniture, stoves, coffins, and agricultural imple-

Jewish immigrant Julius Freyhan, shown with his four daughters, arrived in this country in 1851 and became one of the state's wealthiest men thanks to thriving businesses in Bayou Sara and St. Francisville. Courtesy of the West Feliciana Historical Society.

ments, as well as cotton ginnery. At one point, the Julius Freyhan and Company letterhead proclaimed "wholesale and retail dealers and cotton buyers." One newspaper account referred to J. Freyhan & Co. as "an extensive firm and popular business resort."

The business was considered by no less than the *New York Times* as one of the principle houses on par with Chicago's Marshall Field & Co. In 1896, the handwritten accounts of the Bowman sisters of Rosedown Plantation gave an idea of the huge variety of items stocked at J. Freyhan & Co. Charged to their account were such things as:

a gallon of the best whiskey for three dollars, cartridges, hams, sugar and cocoa, yards of cambric and gingham fabric, olive oil, mustard and cinnamon, hinges, twenty-five peaches at a penny apiece, socks and shirt, a coat and vest, grits, syrup, lunch tongue, buckram, straps and yoke, lap robe, whip, envelopes, spectacles, thread, bacon, lady's tan hose, lace, ribbon, pills, quinine, a linen duster for four dollars, two bottles of champagne at two dollars apiece, jars, soap and brushes, one corset, corn starch, a tub of pure lard, nails, linseed oil and turpentine, cups and saucers, salmon and lobsters, a bucket and an agate pan for forty-five cents together, calico, two waists, and a metallic casket for one hundred dollars.

Impoverished spinsters struggling to hold onto their ancestral home and land, the Bowman sisters lived in an immense Greek Revival mansion without electricity or running water, and their accounts with J. Freyhan & Co., even at these low prices, sometimes ran to a one thousand dollars balance due, with occasional bales of cotton credited toward their debt at the store.

Nevertheless, the success of J. Freyhan & Co. and other stores meant improved living conditions for the merchant families, and the Freyhan family summered at fashionable resorts in places like Newport, Rhode Island, and booked passage on transatlantic steamers. They also engaged in philanthropies to benefit the entire community.

Julius Freyhan, and later his widow, provided the bulk of the funding to construct (and then rebuild after a disastrous fire) the parish's first central public school in 1905, a beautiful brick building with eight rooms and an upper auditorium with ceiling of pressed tin. He was a founding member of the Bayou Sara Lodge #162 of B'nai B'rith. And it was in his opera house in Bayou Sara (back in the days when opera houses were more inclined toward vaudeville than purely operatic productions) that the first organized Jewish congregation came together after meeting initially in the

Meyer Hotel in 1892. In 1893 the group began planning to build a temple, and in 1901 a formal incorporation known as Temple Sinai was set up, with livery stable owner Ben Mann as president of the congregation. Active work began on the building on high ground in St. Francisville in July 1902. Julius Freyhan donated the organ for the temple; his brother-in-law Emanuel Wolf donated the Perpetual Lamp. As was the custom, Freyhan brought to this country his nephew Morris Burgas Jr. to keep the books, buy cotton, and manage cotton warehouses and mercantiles. Born in 1862 and a graduate of the Universites of Berlin and Oxford, Burgas eventually had his own fine general merchandise store by the 1890s in St. Francisville and married into the Rosenthal family.

When Julius Freyhan died at the age of seventy-two in 1904, having suffered "an apoplectic stroke" while on a trip to New York, the New Orleans *Times-Picayune* called him "one of Louisiana's wealthy and enterprising citizens . . . a striking example of a self-made man. He was born . . . in Breslau, Germany, but came to this country very early in life. His first home was Bayou Sara . . . where through his energy and business acumen, he was able to build up one of the largest supply houses in the states." Freyhan had moved his family to St. Charles Avenue in New Orleans and accepted a position as president of Lane Cotton Mills, but, according to the paper, "he also continued his business in Bayou Sara, and until his death was the moving spirit in all of his large interests."

◆◆◆

Another German immigrant, gentile Charles Weydert, had a large hardware store and blacksmith shop in Bayou Sara where he sold farm equipment, tools, housewares, and a little bit of everything. By the end of the nineteenth century he had moved his business up the hill into St. Francisville and had a fine house nearby on Ferdinand Street. Weydert's home was built by Adolph Teutsch, who had arrived in 1880 and also operated a dry goods emporium. Teutsch also oversaw construction of Temple Sinai in 1902 and, like Julius Freyhan and Dietrich Holl, brought from the Old Country a nephew to help in the business (and like Holl, when Teutsch died, nephew Rudolph wed his widow).

Not all of the merchants in early Bayou Sara were Jewish and not all of them were German. One, John McVea, arrived in Louisiana in the 1820s and prospered sufficiently from his store in Bayou Sara to return to Ireland for his family, wife Ellen and son John. When he died in 1831, the exacting inventory of his "General Merchandising firm of John McVea and Rob-

Charles Weydert, at right in suspenders, had a bustling hardware and blacksmith business in Bayou Sara. Courtesy of the West Feliciana Historical Society.

ert Caskaden" included accounts between 1828 and 1831 owing amounts ranging from 38 cents (David Bradford) to $2,893.14 (John Hogan & Co.). Another merchant of Anglo ancestry was James H. Logan, born in 1860 in Bayou Sara of Irish/English parents, who, at age fourteen, had to assume responsibility for his mother and three sisters after the death of his father. He began working at breaking coal for one dollar a day and saved enough that he could build a family home on Principal Street for nine hundred dollars. As an adult, the industrious Mr. Logan served five terms as mayor of Bayou Sara.

In 1862, Alfred Thomas Gastrell, whose occupation in England at age fourteen was listed as "Printer Reader," emigrated with his widowed mother to the United States, served in the Civil War, became an American citizen in 1868, and settled in the Bayou Sara/St. Francisville area, where he built up a thriving business. Advertisements in newspapers from 1884 list "A.T. Gastrell, Bayou Sara, LA, dealer in Hardware, Stoves, Iron and Steel Galvanized Lightning Rods, Smoke Stacks, Breeching etc. made to order. All kinds Engine work; Pipe-cutting; Machine fittings made to order. Tin, Copper and Sheet Iron works. Guttering and Tin roofing to order." He also built bridges and ensured the public safety by repairing jail cells in Pointe Coupee. According to a newspaper account of July 1885 the repair contract for "the cage on the inside of the jail" was awarded by that parish's police jury to A.T. Gastrell of Bayou Sara, promising, "After the completion there will be no more escapes through broken jails."

∽

Before the Civil War, when the 1860 population of Bayou Sara was 540 (360 whites, 152 slaves, and 28 free persons of color), John Francis Irvine Sr. established himself in the port city and for the rest of his life he dominated the Bayou Sara business and political scene. Born in 1828 in Jessamine County of Kentucky, he served as mayor from 1874 to 1898, when he died at age seventy.

As mayor, John F. Irvine Sr. implemented improvements like street-lights and raised wooden sidewalks, developments no doubt greatly appreciated by Bayou Sara residents. Horses and wagons had to plow through the flooded streets when the river rose, but pedestrians could keep their feet dry and continue to patronize the stores via raised walkways. It couldn't have been easy to maintain roads in safe condition. One article in *The Feli-*

Charles Weydert, with daughters Augusta (left) and Gretchen, began with a hardware store and blacksmith shop in Bayou Sara, and later moved his businesses up the hill into St. Francisville safe from the floodwaters. Courtesy of the West Feliciana Historical Society.

Hardware store owner Charles Weydert poses in the open doorway of his blacksmith shop with his wife and baby daughters, along with smithy workers in long leather aprons to protect them from the heat of the open flames. Courtesy of the West Feliciana Historical Society.

The blacksmith shop of Charles Weydert was busy in the days of iron tools, wheels, and horse-drawn conveyances. Courtesy of the West Feliciana Historical Society.

Charles Weydert poses in front of his Bayou Sara home.
Courtesy of the West Feliciana Historical Society.

The Weydert family in Bayou Sara.
Courtesy of the West Feliciana Historical Society.

The crenellated and turreted frame home of mayor John F. Irvine Sr., undoubtedly one of the finest homes in Bayou Sara. Courtesy of the Thomas H. and Joan W. Gandy Photograph Collection, Louisiana and Lower Mississippi Valley Collections, LSU Libraries, Baton Rouge, La.

ciana Sentinel of December 1, 1877, humorously complained,

To have your horse's leg cleverly broken, try the bridge across Principal Street, Bayou Sara, near Firemen's Hall, on a dark night. Every facility is there to be found. If this fails, however, don't despair, but haste to the bridge near the residence of Mrs. Ross in St. Francisville, where your efforts may possibly be crowned with the amplest success. The Street Committee of Bayou Sara and the Road Overseer of the 1ˢᵗ Ward may be 'respectfully invited to attend a funeral.'" Snippets from other newspapers of the 1880s comment on conditions of sidewalks in both towns: "The sidewalks in St. Francisville are in a rather delapidated [*sic*] condition; those of the neighboring town of Bayou Sara are kept in better order.

From 1882 to 1892 Irvine held a lease, for $950 annually, on Bayou Sara's public landing space along the Mississippi River, running along the riverfront between the center of Principal Street and the mouth of Bayou Sara creek, with the exclusive privilege of occupying the same for a wharf boat and collecting docking or wharfage fees of two dollars per day for each steam vessel landing within the limits of Bayou Sara for passengers, freight, mail, supplies, or repairs. Irvine's multiple other business enterprises in Bayou Sara included a steam ferry and tugboat, an icehouse, cotton compress, sawmill, hotel, coal company, liquor and tobacco distributorship, and a general mercantile. The April 9, 1898, edition of the *Democrat* welcomed the addition of Irvine's icehouse: "The ice factory building at the corner of Sun and Front streets in Bayou Sara, opposite the Burton Hotel, is now in the course of erection. The frame was raised this week, and lumber for the building is being rapidly turned out by Irvine's sawmill. Work will be pushed in order to have the plant ready for the warm season. The factory commands a fine situation on the river front. It is a very welcome enterprise, and has every prospect of success."

Fred Hochenedel in 1892 went to work for the firm of John F. Irvine and Son at Bayou Sara and recalled the port as a bustling business center sprawling along the bluff below St. Francisville, with riverboats bringing merchandise downriver from St. Louis and upriver from New Orleans to Irvine and Son's large warehouse. Merchants would come by horse and

Mayor John F. Irvine Sr. had, among his many business enterprises, this enormous ice house which did a bustling business in the days before reliable electrical refrigeration. Note the horse-drawn beer wagon. Courtesy of the Thomas H. and Joan W. Gandy Photograph Collection, acquired from the West Feliciana Historical Society.

Bayou Sara was a busy cotton port in the nineteenth century with commodious hotels like the double-galleried Burton House welcoming steamboat passengers, drummers, and other visitors. Courtesy of the Thomas H. and Joan W. Gandy Photograph Collection, Louisiana and Lower Mississippi Valley Collections, LSU Libraries, Baton Rouge, La.

buggy and with large wagons drawn by yokes of oxen, four or five to a wagon, to pick up goods for resale in their communities. He recalled, "the business life was in Bayou Sara, the social life in St. Francisville. In those days Bayou Sara was a center of activity for the area."

Irvine's first wife was Theresa Ann Burton, born in 1834, whose father, W.F. Burton, had a bustling hotel in Bayou Sara. Drifters and drummers, steamboat passengers, and visitors of every stripe found the double-galleried Burton House accommodating. Her husband would have his own new hotel on the riverfront called Irvine House. They were the parents of seven children, including a son born in 1863 and named for his father.

Bayou Sara mayor John F. Irvine Sr. and his second wife, Emma Henshaw, had two daughters and lived in an elaborately crenellated and turreted frame house just off Principal Street. With bay windows, fanciful trim work, and a picket fence, this was undoubtedly the finest house in town. Their youngest daughter Jessamine was named for the county in Kentucky where her father was born. In 1902, after marrying a young Episcopal clergyman, she died along with the twin sons she was delivering. Mayor Irvine himself saw Bayou Sara recover from fires and Civil War shelling, but blessedly did not live to witness the devastating early 1900s floods; by

1927, when the town's charter was revoked, there was only one registered voter in Bayou Sara.

∽

As the port city of Bayou Sara expanded in the nineteenth century and lumber was in great demand, John F. Irvine Jr. took over his late father's business empire, including the sawmill that by 1912 was turning out 75,000 feet of lumber daily. That year saw the first of the devastating floods of the early 1900s, most notably 1912, 1920, and 1927, from which Bayou Sara and the Irvine empire never recovered.

The flood of 1912 put a foot of water into the second story of Irvinemoor, the late Victorian home of John F. Irvine Jr., who by then had succeeded his father as a successful businessman and politician. Built in 1904, the home had a rounded tower, double galleries, and lots of windows; it was to have been the setting for the wedding of Augusta, the daughter of Irvine's wife Emma Raum Sherrard, his stepmother's niece, whose nuptials had to be moved up the hill to St. Francisville where she married Kemp

John F. Irvine & Son was just one of many family enterprises that included steam ferry and tugboat, icehouse, cotton compress, sawmill, hotel, coal company, tobacco distributorship and general mercantile. Courtesy of the West Feliciana Historical Society.

Man standing by the trunk of a large cypress tree. Because of its cyclical flooding by the Mississippi River, Cat Island swamp, just north of Bayou Sara, has
provided a unique habitat for enormous cypress trees for centuries and no doubt
furnished many of the resources for the Bayou Sara Lumber Company. Courtesy
of the 'Andrew D. Lytle's Baton Rouge' Photograph Collection, Louisiana and
Lower Mississippi Valley Collections, LSU Libraries, Baton Rouge, La.

As the port city expanded in the ninteenth century, Bayou Sara Lumber Company was one of many Irvine family businesses. The sawmill daily was turning out over 75,000 feet of lumber by 1912, when the first devastating flood from which the Irvine empire never recovered hit. Courtesy of the Thomas H. and Joan W. Gandy Photograph Collection, acquired from the West Feliciana Historical Society.

Smith at Hillcroft, the home of Judge Samuel M. Lawrason.

In 1889, according to the Pointe Coupee *Banner*, Irvine was involved in an affair of honor that ended fatally. Said the newspaper account, "As we go to press (January 5, 1889) the report comes to us of a deadly shooting affray in Bayou Sara, on the 3d inst. in which Mr. Thomas Powell, a young man about 20 years of age, a son of Judge S.J. Powell, of the 4th Circuit Court, was shot and killed by Mr. J.F. Irvine, Jr., a younger son of the Mayor of the town. It appears that Irvine met Powell on the street, in front of Alexander's Hotel, and demanded an apology from him on behalf of his father, whom Powell had insulted at Freyhan's Hall on the 31st ult. Powell refused to apologize, and after a few words, drew his pistol and struck Irvine upon the head. Irvine then drew his gun and fired twice. Powell staggered into the hotel and fell dead."

Irvine did not die until 1934, when obituaries referred to him as one-time mayor of Bayou Sara and "outstanding in the lumber business, having been one of the wealthiest lumbermen in the state."

Irvinemoor, late Victorian home of Bayou Sara businessman and politician John F. Irvine Jr, was built in 1904 and destroyed by floodwaters in 1912. Courtesy of the Thomas H. and Joan W. Gandy Photograph Collection, acquired from the West Feliciana Historical Society.

Holding his infant daughter, John F. Irvine Jr. poses in front of his two-horse buggy with his wife Emma Raum Irvine in dark riding outfit, in 1910 in Bayou Sara. Courtesy of the West Feliciana Historical Society.

Other merchants doing business in Bayou Sara, some extrapolated by
Donna B. Adams from the pages of Dun & Bradstreet, others from advertisements in the newspapers of the times, included the following:

William Ball, Apothecary and druggist, front of Bayou Sara landing,
1830; G.B. and F. Enochs, dealers in mausoleums, tombs, monuments,
head and foot stones at Bayou Sara and Baton Rouge; L.T. Maddux,
coach making and repairs; A. Szabo, merchant tailor, Bayou Sara, in the
new house between Charles Hoffmans, Esq.'s home and the new livery
stables of J.H. Honsaw on Principal St.;Bayou Sara & Woodville Telegraph Co.; Conrad Bockel, General Store, Dealer in Fancy and Staple
Goods, & Saddler on Sun Street; A.B. Bryant Saloon; Adam Deckler,
First Class Saloon; M. & A. Fischer, Dry Goods & Groc.; A.T. Gastrell,
Hardware, Stoves, Agricultural implements, etc.; M. Goldman and D.
Rosen, General Store; J.H. Henshaw, Livery; John F. Irvine, Commission
merchant, steamboat agent, etc.; Henry Jacobs and Bro., General Store;
S.N. Lewis, General Store; William H. Mageal, Painter; A. Mann, Gen-
eral Store; Moses Mann, General Store; Martinez, Confectioners etc.;
I. Martinez, Grocery; Raphael Martinez, Cigar Mfg; F.M.Mumford,
Drugs; Picard & Weil, General Store, Highest Market Prices paid for
Cotton; M. Reech, Builder; Reech & Carmouche, Carpenters; D. Rettig,
Baker & Grover; Henrietta Scott, Hotel; Louis Vrensinsky, Shoemaker;
Mrs. E. Weber, General Store; L. Weil, General Store; E.W. Whitman,
Receiving, forwdg. & Steamboat Agent; M & Fischer, southwest corner
Front and Sun Streets, General Merchandise, Bassinet Bars, Parasols,
Victorian Lawns, etc.; F.M. Mumford MD, Chemist, Principal Street;
J.S.Sweetman, General Merchandise and Refreshment Saloon (Foot of
the Hill); John Roth, Fashionable Boot and Shoe Maker; H. Arnaud's
Barber Shop, B.T. White Proprietor, Square Deal Saloon and Billiard
Room; M. Rosenthal, Boots and Shoemaker; Simon Hart, Levee Front,
Wines, Liquors and Cigars.

A preserved bill of sale from 1852 lists Harriet Mathews having purchased 53 7/8 yards of "velvet carpet" for $120 from I. Meyer & Hofman
in Bayou Sara, to cover the cypress flooring of the fine formal Victorian
parlor at Butler Greenwood Plantation, the carpeting being sewn in place
in twenty-seven-inch strips and tacked wall-to-wall with hand-forged
iron tacks. Advertisements for Henry Tenny, "house carpenter and join-
er, Bayou Sara," told of his "Crane's Metalic Patent Burial Casket" at his
shop near J.H. Henshaw's Stable in 1858, while other advertisements of
the time tout "Pachot Gun Maker, Sun Street near the Methodist church,
Bayou Sara; ready-made guns kept on hand for sale," and also "F. Romand,

Bayou Sara, LA, informs his old patrons and the public in general that he has repurchased his Jewelry establishment where he will, as heretofore, endeavor to give complete satisfaction. He has on hand a complete assortment of Watches and Jewelry. Terms Cash."

In 1885, Mme. J. Elise Austin, milliner and dressmaker, advertised a "full line of hats and fancy goods." She even crossed the river from Bayou Sara to New Roads to service patrons on that side of the Mississippi, taking with her "a full supply of hats and trimmings, and will then be prepared to take measurements for dress-making, in which she guarantees a perfect fit."

Many surviving examples of crockery whiskey jugs stenciled with the names of Bayou Sara merchants attest to the practice of barkeeps giving patrons jugs to be brought in and filled over and over, mostly with Kentucky bourbon that was purchased in vast quantities and then sold under individual saloon labels printed on the earthenware jugs.

John Roth, father of Amelia Roth Weydert, is shown in 1912. Courtesy of the West Feliciana Historical Society.

In 1887 it was announced with great excitement that the Bayou Sara Compress Company had been organized, with Morris Wolf, president; Julius Picard, vice president; Wash Hands, secretary-treasurer; and board of directors Duncan Stewart, Isaac T. Hart, H. Rothschild, Judge Thomas Butler, J. Ventress, S.D. Barrow, and J. F. Irvine. The subscription list amounted to over $21,000, and seven lots near the West Feliciana Railroad depot were purchased for shipments and landing. "This is certainly a boom for this little city and in the near future it will no doubt have a national bank and a cotton-seed oil mill," the newspaper account predicted.

Business owners offered a wide variety of goods and services to attract as many customers as possible and meet all needs. Consider the Alexander Hotel, opposite the steamboat landing in Bayou Sara where D. Alexander, the proprietor, advertised this varied assortment of offerings: "Meals at all hours. Hotel open day and night for the accommodation of travelers. Billiard Saloon and First-Class Bar attached. In conjunction with, and adjoining to the hotel is kept D. Alexander's Store with a fine supply of Groceries, Wines and Liquors, Hay, Corn Oats & Bran. No drayage charged. Country orders solicited." W.M. Haile's Drugstore encouraged patronage by giving away free trial bottles of "Dr. King's New Discovery for Consumption;" said an 1887 newspaper posting, "Their trade is simply enormous in this very valuable article from the fact that it always cures and never disappoints. Coughs, Colds, Asthma, Bronchitis, Croup, and all throat and lungs diseases quickly cured. You can test it before buying by getting a trial bottle free. Large size $1. Every bottle warranted."

These merchants of Bayou Sara came from France, Italy, Ireland, England, Hungary, and especially Germany. Bayou Sara census records through the mid- to late 1800s list their skills as: clerks, dry goods merchants, grocers, barbers, physicians, butchers, lawyers, merchants, brick masons, shoemakers, tailors, carpenters, saloonkeepers, bakers, cabinetmakers, millwrights, wagon makers, blacksmiths, stockbrokers, druggists, confectioners, watchmakers, seamstresses, upholsterers; other household members in census records were listed as housekeepers, boarders, widows, and children.

There seemed to be a preponderance of German immigrants in Bayou Sara. Beginning in the seventeenth century, German immigration continued into the late nineteenth century at a rate exceeding that of any other country, according to the *History of German-American Relations-1683-1900-History and Immigration*. Economic problems in Germany brought a whole new wave of immigrants at the beginning of the nineteenth century, with nearly one million German immigrants entering this country in the 1850s. With wages in the United States up to five times higher than those in Europe, most immigrants between 1820 and 1860 came from northern and western Europe, especially after Ireland's potato famine of the 1840s and the unsuccessful 1848 revolution in Germany. This explosion of immigration into the United States nearly tripled the population; between 1820 and 1890 an estimated twenty-eight million immigrants entered this country. New Orleans was the second busiest arrival port, second only to New York, and many of those immigrants made their way up along the Mississippi River corridor, often ending up in Bayou Sara.

The integration of these immigrants into their communities and the affection and respect with which they came to be regarded is seen in a July 1885 obituary for Gus Levi:

> It is our painful duty to chronicle in the *Banner* the sad intelligence of the death of the above-named gentleman, who died in Bayou Sara, West Feliciana parish, La., on 18th inst., after suffering for over a week from a dose of bi-chloride of mercury (poison) he had taken through mistake, thinking it was Hunyadi water, which he was in the habit of taking as a mild purgative. Mr. Levi located in Bayou Sara about two years or more ago, having married Miss Carrie Weil, daughter of the much lamented Simon Weil of that place. He became a partner in the firm of Picard & Weil, and his standing in the commercial world admits of no superior. He was recognized as one of the merchant princes of Bayou Sara, a gentleman of high standing and culture, who was admired for his manly, noble and generous heart. In the relations of life, in which it has been our good fortune to meet Mr. Levi, we have found him to be of that sterling nature which makes the cultured gentleman. In his death, Bayou Sara and the surrounding country has lost one whose place will be hard to fill, either in business or social circle. To the bereaved widow, relatives and friends, we extend our deepest and sincerest sympathy in this, the one great loss of their lives, and pray that God may help them to bear up under their great burden.

By the 1880s and 1890s, the listing of Bayou Sara places of business paying West Feliciana Parish Business Licenses narrowed. The most-listed occupations were merchant, liquor and retail dealer. There were also listings for "2 Stallions and 1 Jack," plus lots of other stallions listed under occupations, evidence of the continued importance of horse-trading. J. Freyhan & Co. had numerous accounts as "Merchants; Liquor & Merchants; Merchant & Retail Liquor; Merchants; Public Gin; Retail Dealer;

Raised wooden walkways let store patrons keep their feet dry while horses and wagons had to plow through the floodwaters as Bayou Sara merchants tried to continue providing services to faithful customers. Courtesy of the West Feliciana Historical Society.

Cotton Gin; Ware House; General Dealers; Gin House," and by the late 1900s these businesses of his were divided between Bayou Sara and St. Francisville as commercial establishments moved up on the bluff away from the floodwaters. The Irvine empire, however, continued listing only Bayou Sara as its place of business in the 1880s and 1890s for "Liquor & Merchant; Retail Merchants; Liquor & Retail Dealer; Wholesale & Retail; Whiskey; Merchant; Saw Mill." But by 1912, John F. Irvine Jr., after being flooded out once too often, salvaged what he could of his elaborate Bayou Sara domicile and rebuilt up on St. Francisville's high bluff overlooking his former home.

Business licenses from 1884 to 1899, as compiled by Ann DeVillier Riffel from records of the parish tax collector, show that a number of the Bayou Sara business owners had multiple interests and are as follows:

Alexander, D and Mrs. D: merchant, bar room, 2 billiard tables; B.S. Lumber Co.: lumber; C.W. Ball: retail dealer; Dr. A.F. Barrow: MD; C.M. Barrow: 2 stallions & 1 jack; Col. Hilliard Barrow: 1 stallion; N.H. Barrow: 1 stallion; Bayou Sara Lumber Co: wharfboat, sawmill, receiving and forwarding; Conrad Bockel and Mrs. B. Bockel: merchant, liquor and retail dealer; Boyalski: bar and table; L.C. Bradley: physician; Mrs. M. Brandon: liquor and retail dealer; S. Brasseux: liquor merchant; J.B.

Sorry Sansoni's store when the Levee first broke.

Levee breaks sent the Sansoni grocery, operated by Italian immigrant Frank Sansoni, up the hill into St. Francisville by 1910. Courtesy of the West Feliciana Historical Society.

Brooks: retail liquor; E.A. Brown: merchant; Gus Brown: merchant; John Brown: retail dealer; S.J. Brown: liquor merchant; Dr. W.W. Burkhalter: MD; H.R. Camp: merchant; Zack Cavalier: 1 stallion; M. Cochran: whiskey, merchandise; M. Cohen & Co.: merchandise; Converse Bros.: 2 stallions; E.W. Converse: retail dealer; W.R. Daniels: retail dealer; Eli Davis: 1 stallion; Adam Deckler: bar room and merchant; Chris Dedon: retail merchant; Forest Douglas: 1 stallion; J.D. Dum: tin shop; Valentine Emery: 1 stallion; A.S.J. Evans: 1 stallion; B. Farley: merchant and retail dealer; Jack Fields: merchant and retail dealer; M.&A. Fischer: merchant; J. Freyhan & Co.: liquor and merchant, public gin, cotton gin, warehouse, gin house, merchandise, retail liquor and merchandise, etc.; S.A. Friar: retail dealer; Gus Friend: billiards and retail dealer, pool table; Felix Gabriel: merchant, liquor and retail dealer; A.L. Gastrell: merchant, hardware merchant; Warren A. Gay: 1 stallion; George & George: peddlers; Joseph Goldman: liquor and merchant, retail dealer; A.C. Gore: lumber; Dr. A.C. Gore: dentist; A. Harris: merchant, liquor and retail dealer, merchandise; B. Harris: merchant; William Hartson: merchant and retail dealer; Ellis Hilliard: 1 stallion; Howell & Percy: liquor and merchant, retail dealer; John F. Irvine, J.F. Irvine & Son: liquor and retail merchants, whiskey, saw mill; Joseph John: merchant; H.C. Kaufman:

merchandise, whiskey; Kilbourne & Co.: merchant, druggist; J.N. Labry: baker; Lajune Bros.: merchant; Louis Leahaman: retail dealer; Dr. James Leake: MD; W.W. Leake: attorney at law; L. Lehman: merchant; P.&.J. LeJeune: retail merchant; T. Leonard: livery stable; Jos. Levi: merchants; M.C. Levy: merchant; Dr. H. Lofton: dentist; H.C. Lopez: 1 stallion; J.L. Lyons & Co.: drugstore; Mann & Levy: retail dealer, merchant; Ben Mann: liquor and merchant; Max Mann: merchant and retail liquor; H. Marks: peddler; L. Marks: merchant and liquor, retail dealer, merchandise and whiskey; Fred Marks: peddler; H. Martin: merchant and retail liquor; Kimp Mattingly: liquor and retail dealer; D.F. Merwin: liquor and retail dealer; Joe Meyer: liquor and merchant, retail dealer; Mrs. C. Mitchell: liquor and retail dealer; Mumford & Brooks: merchant, liquor and drugs; F.H.J. Mumford: druggist; T.M. Mumford: merchant; E. Nasiff: merchant; Geo. Nasiff: merchant and retail liquor; E. Newman: merchant and retail dealer; E.L. Newsham: retail dealer and merchant; Henry Pate: 1 stallion; Mrs. H. B. Perkins: merchant and liquor; W.C. Perkins: merchant and liquor; Picard & Picard: merchant; Picard & Weil: merchant; Julius Picard: merchant, livery stable; George Plettinger: bar room, liquor and retail dealer, merchant; J. G. Plettinger: bar

In 1918, the view up the hill into high-and-dry St. Francisville tempted many Bayou Sara merchants to abandon the flood-prone port city and move their businesses onto the bluff. Courtesy of the West Feliciana Historical Society.

room, 1 billiard table, merchant and liquor; M.A. Porter: 1 stallion; Dr. Sidney Powell: dentist; J.W. Prather: merchant; C.H. Reid: 2 stallions; D. Rittig: bar room; Newton Robinson: 1 stallion; Geo. Russel: merchandise; Geo. Schlesenger: merchant; Nat Smith: 1 stallion; Charles Spencer: liquor and retail dealer; Joseph Stein: merchant; Joseph Stern: liquor and merchant, livery stable; Mrs. M.H. Stern: merchant; William Stewart: liquor and retail dealer; Virgil Stirling: 1 stallion; E.S. Swartz: peddler; L.C.Szaba: retail liquor, merchandise, whiskey; David Taylor: retail dealer; Dr. W.H. Taylor: MD; C.W. Tempel: liquor and merchant, retail dealer; H.W. Temple: liquor and retail dealer; Walter Templet: merchant; F.H. Tenney: liquor and merchant; Louis Teutsch: liquor and retail dealer; A. Teutsch: merchant; F.H. Tinney: liquor and retail dealer; Miss H. Townes: retail dealer; Villeret & Allain: druggist; Jim Vinci: merchant; Charles Weydert: merchandise; Dr. Whittington: physician; O.P. Worthy: liquor and retail dealer; Ollie Worthy: 1 stallion.

5

Early Travel

In the nineteenth century, travels to St. Francisville and its sister city Bayou Sara beneath the bluffs were fraught with perils and gave rise to some spectacularly gruesome newspaper dispatches.

There were rough early roadways through the wilderness, along which the initial settlement patterns could be traced. The pioneers of the late eighteenth and early nineteenth centuries braved attacks by Indians, bandits, and wild animals as they descended the Natchez Trace into what was then Spanish territory to carve the early indigo and cotton plantations from the Feliciana wilderness.

Even the main street of St. Francisville through the 1800s was the scene of cattle drives and heavy-laden mule-drawn wagons en route to the riverport at Bayou Sara. Muddy quagmires during wet weather and deeply rutted the rest of the time, these roadways led to some unfortunate accidents, buggies bouncing and overturning, with runaway horses compounding the problems. One of the earliest burials at historic Grace Episcopal Church, on the road leading through St. Francisville to the river, was that of baby Edward Baldwin, just five months old, whose cause of death in 1840 was listed as "flung from buggy," a not-uncommon occurrence.

And then there were the steamboat explosions, sinkings, and wrecks, such as the February 1859 catastrophe of the steamboat *Princess*, which nearly decimated the Feliciana bar. Having boarded passengers at the Bayou Sara landing, the fast packet was headed to New Orleans for the opening of the state Supreme Court and was packed with over two hundred prominent passengers. Delayed by fog upriver, the boat was running behind schedule and its crew stoked the blazing fires and tried to make up for lost time. When the *Princess* exploded at Conrad's Point just below Baton Rouge, over seventy passengers were mortally wounded. Conrad family slaves pulled badly burned survivors from the river waters and rolled them in barrels of flour to ease their agony.

The New Orleans *Times-Picayune* of March 8, 1859, ran this account of the impact of the explosion of the *Princess* on the community of Bayou Sara:

A cattle drive down Ferdinand Street in St. Francisville going to Bayou Sara. Courtesy of the West Feliciana Historical Society.

The State in Mourning: Our numerous exchanges from the interior of the State come to us this morning in deep mourning at the late dreadful disaster, which has brought desolation and woe to so many happy homes. There is scarcely a community from which someone of the lost is not missing, or to it known by his social virtues. Among the greatest sufferers is the flourishing village of Bayou Sara, which mourns the loss of four of its most prominent and worthy citizens: Messrs. Seymour H. Lurty, L.D. Brewer, Henderson C. Hudson and U.B. Phillips. Mr. Lurty was one of the most widely known citizens of the parish, of which he had been Sheriff for more than seventeen years. Honest and faithful in every duty he was known, indeed, throughout the State as 'the model officer.' He was about forty-five years of age, in the prime of life, and leaves a wife and two children to mourn his untimely fate. Mr. Brewer was also an old esteemed citizen of the parish and stood at the head of the bar as a jury lawyer. None stood higher, indeed, in the community generally, and no one had truer and warmer friends. He likewise leaves an amiable wife and several young promising children. Mr. Hudson also ranked high in his profession, besides being distinguished for his general scholarship and many social virtues. He, too, was a man of family, and in the prime of life. Saturday morning, when the *Ledger* was issued, Mr. Phillips was still alive, but there was little prospect of his surviving long. The whole community was in mourning. Messrs. C. D. Smith and G. Merrick Miller of Bayou Sara were also on board the *Princess*, but miraculously escaped.

Passengers boarded these riverboats with not a little fear and trepidation despite the fact that many of the steamboats were floating palaces offering commodious cabins and sumptuous meals. Luxurious as they were for passenger travel at the time, the steamboats were far from reliable or safe means of transportation, vulnerable as they were to mid-river fires and explosions, snags, sinkings, floods, and other perils of river traffic. This was especially true because speed was so important. The quicker the cotton shipments reached factors in New Orleans for sale, the better, because whole plantation empires depended on the sale of the crop for their livelihood from year to year, and price fluctuations could mean the difference between profit and loss. The boats raced up and down the river, the swiftest winning contracts to deliver mail, cotton, and trade goods, sometimes throwing caution to the winds.

The newspapers of the day were rarely governed by the dictates of good taste and proper political correctness, and journalists had a field day coming up with ever-more scintillating stories of trials and tragedies in order to sell papers. One of the more flamboyant accounts appeared in an extra edition of the *Louisiana Chronicle*, headlined "Bayou Sara, LA Steamer *Clipper No. 1* Explosion, September 1843," quoting extensively from the

The *Duncan F. Kenner*, built in 1859 and burned in 1860, made three weekly roundtrips between Bayou Sara and New Orleans. It was named for an Ashland Plantation sugar planter who supported emancipation but was a Confederate emissary to Europe. Courtesy of the West Feliciana Historical Society, Peter W. Patout Collection.

New Orleans *Picayune*; even the *Brooklyn Daily Eagle* in New York carried the story. Although only fourteen persons were killed, ten others missing and feared dead, and nine wounded, the article calls this "one of the most terrible catastrophies [*sic*] which has ever happened on the Mississippi." As the *Clipper No. 1* was backing from her moorings at the Bayou Sara landing bound for Tunica, she blew up

> with an explosion that shook earth, air and heaven, as though the walls of the world were crumbling to pieces about our ears. All the boilers bursting simultaneously—machinery, vast fragments of the boilers, huge beams of timber, furniture and human beings in every degree of mutilation, were alike shot up perpendicularly many hundred fathoms in the air.
>
> On reaching the greatest height [and as the writer reached equally great heights of lurid description] the various bodies diverged like the jets of a fountain in all directions, falling to the earth and upon roofs of houses, in some instances as much as 250 yards from the scene of destruction. The hapless victims were scalded, crushed, torn, mangled and scattered in every possible direction, many into the river, some in the streets, some on the other side of the Bayou nearly 300 yards—some torn asunder by coming in contact with pickets and posts, and others shot like cannon balls through the solid walls of houses at a great distance from the boat.

Local physicians and residents rushed to the scene to help. "Our citizens generally, every man and mother's son, appeared only anxious as to how they might render most service to the poor sufferers—white and black, without distinction." Said the newspaper reporter, "The scene was such as we hope never to look upon again." Fortunately there were no passengers on board, but of the forty-three-man crew, all but nine were killed or "so shockingly mutilated that their lives are despaired of." Even more incredibly, the newspaper account continues, "The watchman, a white man, was thrown alive 100 yards, through the solid wall of Baker's hotel, into a bed. He retained his senses perfectly for some time after, but the poor fellow expired during the evening. The cabin boy was thrown about two hundred yards through the roof of a shed, and was picked up in a mangled condition."

A dispatch of September 29, 1851, from the *New Orleans Crescent* heralded "Steamboat Explosion—Destruction of the *Brilliant*—-Great Loss of Life." The *Brilliant,* bound for Bayou Sara from New Orleans, blew up at Bayou Goula when her second starboard boiler exploded, carrying away the main cabin and staterooms as far aft as the ladies' cabin, and everything forward of the boilers, completely wrecking the boat above the hull. The captain said he'd had up to a hundred deck hands and firemen on board at the time of the explosion, and could find less than a quarter of that number afterward, not to mention the loss of life among the passengers. Survivors were listed as "slightly scalded" or "badly scalded." And, in June of 1851, newspapers carried accounts of the indictments against officers of the steamboat *Echo*, which had recently exploded at Bayou Sara.

In 1867, the headlines read: "Terrible Steamboat Disaster: Burning of the steamer *Fashion* on the Mississippi River; Many Passengers Burned and Drowned—the Pilot, Engineer, Second Mate and Steward among the Lost—Fearful Scene—Panic among the Deck Passengers." The disaster occurred about seven miles above Baton Rouge because of sparks from the chimney, and the fire spread with such rapidity that efforts to check it were of no avail. The *Fashion* had on board 2,700 bales of cotton, adding to the fury of the flames, said the dispatch of January 2, 1867. Cabin passengers were said to number over a hundred; the deck passengers were described as "nearly all Negroes." The dispatch reported that

> the people, to escape the flames, ran backwards and forwards, scarcely knowing whither, until driven into a more compact mass, when they would leap overboard and perish. The pilot remained at his post until driven off by the flames, when he walked to the stern and was not seen afterward. . . . Capt. Pratt saved several ladies by wading waist deep into the river, putting them into a yawl, and paddling it with a portion of the stateroom blinds. The ladies were from Mississippi. Capt. Pratt was almost dead from exhaustion, but finally succeeded in reaching Baton Rouge. . . . A lady passenger threw her three children into the river and then leaped after them. The mother and one of the children were afterward rescued, but the two other children were seen no more. The panic on board the steamer was fearful. . . . The elegantly dressed ladies who came on board at Bayou Sara were among the lost.

When an 1879 hurricane blew ashore and caused tremendous damage along the coast and inland, it came right up the Mississippi River to Bayou Sara, where barges were sunk with loss of cargo, houses were blown down, gins and cotton warehouses demolished, cane leveled and ruined, and trains derailed. The steamboat *Trenton*, having made fast to the bank to hurriedly discharge passengers, went adrift and sank, taking with it eighty-eight bales of cotton, one hundred head of cattle, and all the passengers' belongings.

The river steamer *J.M. White* loaded with cotton, ca. 1895-1901. Besides an ornate salon with a capacity of 350 passengers, the elegant *J.M. White* could carry some 7,000 bales of cotton. Courtesy of the 'Andrew D. Lytle's Baton Rouge' Photograph Collection, Louisiana and Lower Mississippi Valley Collections, LSU Libraries, Baton Rouge, La.

And then there was the 1886 demise of the *J.M. White*, called one of the most glamorous steamboats on the Mississippi in the late nineteenth century. With eighty-one-foot chimneys, a five-tone whistle, and steam-powered loading machinery, she was a side-wheel, wooden hull packet 321 feet long, 91 feet wide, with 10 boilers, and a capacity of 350 salon passengers and 7,000 cotton bales. It was said that few boats on the river could match the technological innovations on board and none could match her speed. Ornate and luxurious, she had a 233-foot-long main cabin with filigree woodwork that could comfortably seat 250 passengers for meals, with twenty-three staterooms on each side of the grand salon. On the top deck, or Texas deck, there were fifty staterooms that were ten by fourteen feet, plus officers' accommodations. There were also two bridal suites.

Launched in 1878, she went up in flames one evening of December 1886 while docked at St. Maurice Plantation above Bayou Sara, the glare illuminating the river for miles. Dozens of cabin passengers, who had retired for the evening, were lost, along with cabin boys, cooks, chambermaids, deckhands, rousters, "three white peddlers," deck passengers, 3,500 bales of cotton, 9,000 sacks of seed, and 200 barrels of oil, plus "the big

Mardi Gras ox, Otoe Chief, six years old and 4,000 pounds. And a man in charge of the fat ox." The fire was said to have probably originated "in the careless moving of some of the deck passengers." Capt. John Irvine Jr. with the tug *Beverly Harris* rendered "valuable services to the unfortunates." One watchman on duty when the *White* was burned said the entire crew "had been suspicious of a disaster during the entire trip."

The New Orleans *Times-Democrat* of December 15, 1886, carried the story, headlined "A River Horror; Another Human Holocaust on the Mississippi; the Steamer *J.M. White* Burned To the Water's Edge With a Great Loss of Life and Property; Terrible Scenes During the Conflagration; Over Forty Persons Known To Have Perished; Sickening Details of a Night of Horrors; Many Leap Into the River to Escape the Flames and Are Drowned." The dispatch from Bayou Sara waxed poetic in describing the terrible tragedy, the reader undoubtedly experiencing the horror as if right on the scene:

The moon was not high above the fringe of woods that lay behind the fields back of the Blue Store, on the Mississippi, in the parish of Pointe Coupee. The steamer *J.M. White* was at the bank, and by the light of pitch pine torches the roustabouts were carrying on board sacks of cotton seed. A large quantity had been already loaded and the work of finishing the shipment was progressing nicely. The cabin lights had been turned down low, most of the cabin passengers had retired to their staterooms, and, save the noise of escaping steam and the footfalls of the crew along the gangway, there was hardly a sound to disturb the perfect quiet. There are but few houses along the shore, and their inmates had retired some time before.

Suddenly the engine was heard to start and the pump began to throw water. Then came a cry of 'fire' and curling out of the engine-room, rolled a thin cloud of smoke. The great bell of the boat began to ring loudly. There was confusion on deck, consternation in the cabin. The smoke grew denser, and from between the bales of cotton in the engine-room flames licked out, devouring whatever came within their reach. The passengers were hurriedly aroused and in their night clothes sought the main hall of the cabin to escape. A thick, choking smoke rendered all objects invisible, and groping about some found their way forward, others found fresh air at the little gallery in the rear.

There came a great yellow light that turned the waters into a flood of gold and lit up the fields and forests for miles around. Men from the upper deck lowered themselves down to the tiers of cotton that lined

The dining room of the *J.M. White*. The nineteenth-century paddle-wheelers were floating palaces, with dining salons serving multi-coursed feasts with white-jacketed waiters. Courtesy of the Thomas H. and Joan W. Gandy Photograph Collection, Louisiana and Lower Mississippi Valley Collections, LSU Libraries, Baton Rouge, La.

the guards, and ran forward toward the stage to escape ashore. Deck passengers below, wild with excitement, hurried this way and that among the cotton bales, seeking egress. Then there were loud cries in the ladies' cabin, shrieks of terror on deck. The crackling of the flames, the roar of the boat, the yells of those already on shore to the unfortunates still on board, gave to the scene more terrors.

The flames now rose above the cabin, near the wheel, and those nearest the stern were cut off from escape. Some leaped into the water. A father and mother threw their little daughter into the arms of the Mississippi; they followed. At the turn the sailorman, Andy Pierson, and a colored man had cut the yawl loose, and with heroic endeavor were plying between the boat and shore, rescuing a freight of souls each trip. Undaunted by the heat and smoke they went back and forth until they could rescue no more. A struggling form was battling in the river, and now and again, above the roar, there came to the affrighted people on the banks his piteous appeals for help and none were able to give him succor.

Frenzied with fright, a crowd of men, women and children were huddled together on the little gallery at the stern of the boat. The lurid glare from the advancing flames gave a ghastly color to their faces. Each stateroom window was aglow with light, as if there was some wild scene

One of the most luxurious steamboats on the Mississippi in the late nineteenth century, the sidewheeler *J.M. White* had an ornate main cabin that could comfortably seat 250 passengers for meals. Courtesy of the Thomas H. and Joan W. Gandy Photograph Collection, Louisiana and Lower Mississippi Valley Collections, LSU Libraries, Baton Rouge, La.

of revelry within the cabin. The heat grew more intense. The cries of help from those doomed ones became louder. Some looked over their shoulders at the devouring monster that came sweeping toward them, and, with a shriek of terror leaped into the water. Others hesitated. They were beyond self control. Dazed, bereft of sense, they screamed but did not move. Then the hot breath of the flames swept past them and they fell back into the seething mass of fire, and no sound came from the little gallery.

The whole heavens were now aglow. The long stretch of river was lit up almost as by sunlight. The country for miles was bright in the effulgent light. Lanes and country roads showed their ruts and holes and trees cast black shadows. Then there came a deep, sullen report of an explosion, and some twenty bales of cotton shot up in the air like blazing meteors, revolving in the flight and falling into the tawny water. Another explosion from the magazine where there was stored some powder followed, blowing the burning timbers in every direction and partially subduing the fire.

The calls for help were now silenced, the voices of the flames alone were heard, and then quivering as if both to give up their post the tottering chimneys leaned over and with a crash fell into the fiery furnace below, sending up a corusacation of sparks. The *J.M. White* was expiring. The cabin had fallen in; the wheelhouse had melted away, and there was now left nothing but the bare hull, a bed of fiery embers, entombing the remains of those who half an hour before were buoyant with hopes and busy dreaming of some happy future that seemed to lie beyond the horizon.

On the shore the survivors looked upon the closing scene almost mute in their consternation. They asked for this one and that; called the names of those they could recollect. One suggested that such a one was missing, another added someone else's name, until at least a few of the lost were counted. The crowd upon the bank were huddled together, gazing with a strange fascination upon the charnel furnace as if loath to leave the spot. The steamer *Stella Wilde* then approached and broke the horrid spell and the survivors left the scene.

∞

The wreck of the *Corona* in October of 1889 was one of the most vivid dispatches from Bayou Sara. A number of survivors reached New Orleans by train,

and as they stepped from the train they were surrounded by a crowd of weeping men and women, all anxious to learn the fate of some loved ones. Capt. Sweeny, who was among them, stated that the whole thing

"SOLID CATTLE TRAIN—WEST FELICIANA DID IT"

The photograph from which this cut was made was taken in Bayou Sara, October 29, 1915, at which time a solid train load of cattle was shipped over the L. R. & N. to Texas points. There were in the train, averaging thirty-two head to the car. The inscription appearing over this cut appeared on large signs attached to the train. The cattle industry in West Feliciana has grown greatly s

Newspaper clipping (from Silver Anniversary issue of *The Democrat*, St. Francisville) showing cattle being shipped by rail from Bayou Sara. Courtesy of the West Feliciana Historical Society.

came on so suddenly that he hardly had time to see anything. Capt. Blanks, who was sitting in the barber's chair, was hurled through the cabin roof and instantly killed. The others in the cabin were struck by flying timbers. Those who were not killed by flying timbers were pinned down and scalded to death. Capt. Sweeny, when the explosion took place, was on the forecastle and thus escaped the heavy timbers that were flying around. He remained on the wreck as long as possible, and as there was no chance to rescue anyone, he sprang overboard and was picked up by the yawl of the *City of St. Louis*.

Steamboat explosions, unavoidable facets of life when travel and transport centered around the Mississippi River, occurred with such distressing regularity that it was a wonder journeys were ever undertaken in those days, and it is a real tribute to the courage and determination of the early residents of Bayou Sara and St. Francisville that they had ever arrived or moved about at all. The unreliability of boat traffic, combined with the coming of the railroad, signaled the beginning of Bayou Sara's demise, bringing an accompanying decrease in river traffic.

∽∾

Then the mainstay of the local economy, cotton, fell into a decline due to the ravages of disease and the boll weevil as well as crop failures and price fluctuations, signaling the inevitable collapse of the plantation system, which actually opened the way for the rise of the business class.

Modern-day replicas of nineteenth-century riverboats like the steam-powered *Delta Queen* still ply the waters of the Mississippi and dock at Bayou Sara for visits to historic St. Francisville. Courtesy of the West Feliciana Historical Society.

Even before the Civil War there were factors beyond the control of the planters that severely impacted production—this included the dreaded yellow fever epidemics, which could decimate a labor force. There were times when steamboats were not allowed to stop at Bayou Sara, the fear being that a passenger would disembark carrying yellow fever; quarantines were put into effect during the worst outbreaks, and boards of health along the river parishes placed inspectors on some steamers to protect against infection and reassure residents that measures were being taken to guard their interests and prevent any feeling of alarm, "which so often endangers the health interest as well as business interest of a community." When epidemics spread through New Orleans, according to one issue of the *Western Journal of Medicine and Surgery*, refugees rushed to Bayou Sara and the vicinity as a retreat from disease, just as others went to Gulf Coast resort areas like Isle Dernier thinking the sea breeze healthy. As regular packets continued trips as usual, cases of yellow fever were introduced with the infected district often starting near the steamboat landing, then spreading among the resident population and even into the countryside.

One dispatch to the *Times-Picayune* of New Orleans dated October 9, 1855, reported:

> I have heard nothing talked of but yellow fever. . . . The whole community of this vicinage seems to be in melancholy gloom. The disease having spread into the country among the negroes so unexpectedly to the planters, who have heretofore been exempted from such an infection, greatly increased the general alarm. On some large plantations as many as sixty cases have occurred among the slave population . . . and it has been doing its work at Bayou Sara, St. Francisville, Pointe Coupee, Jackson and Woodville. . . . The state of affairs retards the shipments of cotton that otherwise could be made.

The cotton industry managed to survive wars and droughts, changing labor patterns, and mechanization, but it was almost wiped out by little beetles with long curving snouts that, in 1892, crossed the Rio Grande from Mexico either by wagon or windstorm and started working their way across the cotton fields of Texas. Within thirty-five years the boll weevil infestation had spread all the way to the Atlantic, devastating cotton fields along the way as the females deposited their eggs in the tender bolls that were then eaten by the young weevils. Desperate farmers would hang huge sacks of calcium arsenate over the backs of mules to dust fields and try to save their crops, but it would not be until the World War II era that the discovery of DDT and effective dispersal methods like crop dusters would allow the implementation of a full-scale boll weevil eradication program. By then, devastating fires and floods had finished off what was left of Bayou Sara.

6

Floods & Fires

The threat of fire was a constant companion. Old newspaper accounts record its frequent recurrence among wood-frame structures heated with wood fires and lit by coal oil and candles. The listings of businesses and homes lost give a clear idea of the variety of commercial operations in Bayou Sara, the closeness of homes to the commercial structures, and the losses suffered by those with no insurance.

The *New York Daily Times* of June 21, 1855, reports in a dispatch from New Orleans, "The town of Bayou Sara has been nearly destroyed by fire. Loss, half a million of dollars."

The New Orleans *Times-Picayune* of the previous day, June 20, 1855, reports under the headline "The Great Fire at Bayou Sara":

We have already given some account of the disastrous fire at Bayou Sara on Friday night, the 14th inst. We have been favored with the following list of the names of the sufferers, and amount insured, showing as near an estimate as possible of the extent and particulars of this great calamity:

Leake & Co, two warehouses, no insurance; E. Hills, coffee house, no insurance; A. Levy, dry good store, $16,000; Charles Hofman & Co. Dry good store, part'y insured; P. Adolphus, grocery store, no insurance; John C. Ferny, tailor, no insurance; A Zabo, tailor, no insurance; E. Hills, dwelling, no insurance; J. Morkel, shoe store, partly insured; J. Garksdull, tin store, no insurance; James Marks, *Ledger* office, no insurance; J. Woodflin, dwelling, no insurance; P. Adolphus, dwelling, no insurance; D.L. Stocking, dentist, no insurance; Mrs. A. Grisham, millinery, no insurance; J. Bockel, saddler, no insurance; L. Gerlaehi, saddler, part'y insurance; F. Woodflin, shoe store, no insurance; J.J. Mayer, dwelling, no insurance; H. Levy & Brother, dry goods store, partly insured; Charles Storr, confectionary, bar room and dwelling; Felix Roman, jewelry, no insurance; Gertrude Nolesco, f.w.c., house vacant, no insurance; Hampton Whitaker, hotel, no insurance; Jacob Mebwel (?), dry good store, no insurance; H.B. Vibbert, drug store, no insurance; Charles E. Tooram, dry good store and two warehouses, $7,000; J. Whitman & Co., warehouse, partly insured; J.B. Harper & Son, drug store, no insurance;

Gertrude Nolasco, dwelling, no insurance; John F. Irvine, dwelling, no insurance; Charles Hofman, dwelling, no insurance; L. Clause, ice house, insurance; James Hale, hotel (Smith's Hotel), no insurance; R. Mumford, warehouse, occupied by M. Crindell, $3,500; P. Wittie, bar room, no insurance; E.P. Bugby, fruit store, partly insured; Lebret & Hearsell, dry good store, $10,000; Marshall House, post-office and telegraph, no insurance; John H. Henshaw, three stables, $1,500; Smith stables. Total loss, $500,000. In addition to the above we have heard of a number of other losses, among which are J.B. & E. Enoch's tombstone warehouse; Whiteman & Hatch, loss $3,000; J.H. Henshaw, loss $8,000; McGinn, dry good store. Two lives lost, James Butler and Frank Dormalley.

Apparently a number of benefits were held to assist those who suffered devastating losses. The July 13, 1855, *Times-Picayune* of New Orleans mentioned an upcoming performance by a group with the catchy name of the Amateur Ethiopian Minstrels, to be held for the benefit of victims of the Bayou Sara fires. There were undoubtedly others as well.

On November 2, 1880, a special from Bayou Sara to the *New Orleans Times*:

A fire broke out in Picard and Weil's stables at 3 o'clock on Sunday morning, destroying a whole square of buildings. The following merchants are burned out: L. Martinez, J.F. Irvine, Kauffman & Miller, Picard & Weil, A Deckler, M. Alexander, Simon Hart and Brown & Co. The telegraph office was also destroyed. The loss is estimated at $200,000. The fire was the work of an incendiary. Telegraphic communication has been restored.

From the *Feliciana Sentinel* of November 6, 1880:

Recently our friend Mr. Jno. F. Irvine, of Bayou Sara has been the especial victim of misfortunes. Not two months since his wharfboat was struck and was only saved by the utmost exertions of the citizens of Bayou Sara. Then came the fire of last Sunday, destroying over two hundred sacks of oats, corn, and an immense lot of flour and other provisions just stored, and again on Thursday night last the steamer *Natchez* in landing at his wharf stove the same against an obstruction and sprung several large leaks which were stopped only after several hours hard work by the good people of Bayou Sara.

And on August 28, 1886, another disastrous fire was reported:

Bayou Sara . . . was burned at an early hour yesterday. The total loss is estimated at over $118,000. The principal sufferers are Frahan & Co. [no doubt a misspelling of J. Freyhan & Co.], loss on stock and building, $100,000; insurance, $75,000. M. Brasseaux, loss on building, $4,000; insurance, $1,000. Kilburn & Co. druggists, building destroyed; goods saved, but badly damaged. Mrs. Deutschland, milliner, store destroyed but stock saved. W.H. Taylor, loss $500; in insurance. F.B. Teutsch, loss on stock, $3,500; insurance, $2,000. William Conn, dwelling and store destroyed; loss, $3,000; insurance, $1,100. Mrs. L. Weil, three stores burned; loss, $4,000; insurance, $2,800. The fire broke out at 1 a.m. There is no doubt that it was of incendiary origin.

Added a report in the Pointe Coupee *Banner*, "all were burnt flat to the ground. Nothing was saved; no lives lost. The fire commenced at Freyhan's store and is supposed to be the work of an incendiary.

And again on May 3, 1888, "A large steam ginnery belong to J. Frey-hart & Co. [J. Freyhan & Co.], together with 1,000 sacks of seed and 500 boxes of coal, was burned Tuesday night at Bayou Sara. Loss, $8,000; insurance, $5,000."

Poor Julius Freyhan suffered another loss in July of 1894, when it was reported that "a very disastrous fire occurred at Bayou Sara near the foot of the hill. Seven or eight large stores were burnt and many other buildings, including Freyhan's warehouse near the river. Twenty-five thousand dollars would not cover the loss. The fire is said to have originated in a kitchen near the railroad depot."

∞

Just as disastrous as the raging fires were the spring floods, for Bayou Sara sat right on the banks of the Mississippi River, and a raging torrent of water raced downstream as ice and snow melted upriver each spring. A reliable levee system was not in place in the nineteenth century, and what levees there were often developed crevasses through which the waters rushed, destroying homes and fields, crops and railroad tracks, and everything else that stood in their path. The aftermath of the flooding also caused its own problems.

In July of 1844 the *New York Tribune* ran a dispatch from the *Bayou Sara Ledger* reporting that the port city, "with the exception of the squares fronting immediately on the river, between the Bayou Sara and Principal street, is fairly inundated. Some families have already left their dwellings, and others are preparing to follow. Altogether, the prospect is uncomfortable enough, for when the water leaves us, the action of the sun on the

The steeple of Bayou Sara's Methodist Church, built in 1844, rises above the floodwaters. Its upper galleries provided refuge for townsfolk during floods until the congregation in 1899 moved up the hill into St. Francisville. Courtesy of the West Feliciana Historical Society.

deposit of vegetable and other matter will scarcely fail to produce death-dealing pestilence among our citizens. It will be a miracle if they escape." In 1851, the *Times-Picayune* of New Orleans reported that the levee at Bayou Sara was to be raised two feet.

Dispatches were sent from New Orleans on April 21, 1890, to the *New York Times*: "Bayou Sara Under Water . . . Several Buildings Washed Away and More Breaks in the Levees." The article described the break in the levee early one morning, inundating the entire town of Bayou Sara with two to seven feet of water, washing several buildings off their foundations. Across the river in Pointe Coupee Parish, a crevasse of some three hundred feet in width opened, and other levee breaks were reported all along the riverbanks as far south as New Orleans, as well.

By the following day's newspaper, the headlines read, "Louisiana's Great Peril: Thousands of Miles of Plantations Under Water; Many Streets in New Orleans Flooded from Lake Pontchartrain—The Morganza Levee Breaks." The news was bad:

Mudboxes and raised wooden walkways were no match for the devastation of the Mississippi River's strong currents when floodwaters sometimes twenty or thirty feet deep rampaged through the streets of Bayou Sara. Courtesy of the West Feliciana Historical Society.

The flood situation has changed rapidly for the worse during the last twenty-four hours, and the condition of affairs was never gloomier or more threatening than it is at present. For the last three days the crest of the great wave in the Mississippi has been passing from Vicksburg down, and the most extraordinary efforts have been made to hold the levees against the high water. A levee relief boat has gone to the scene of danger with supplies, material and men.

In Pointe Coupee and West Baton Rouge 8,000 men have been at work for several days, strengthening the levees, and between here and Bayou Sara probably 20,000 more have been trying to hold the line of dikes; but the rain and wind storm which came on yesterday, coupled with the high water, overthrew all these preparations, and in the last twenty-four hours no less than fifteen breaks have occurred. At Bayou Sara, a town of about ten thousand people, 160 miles above here [New Orleans], the water rose to the first floors of all the stores and houses, put a stop to all business, and compelled the abandonment of the town by the majority of the population.

The resilience of Bayou Sara's residents and merchants was tested by almost yearly flooding, but they considered it a price worth paying for the privilege of living right along the nineteenth century's most used transportation corridor, the Mississippi River. Courtesy of the West Feliciana Historical Society.

The dispatch described the break in the levee at Morganza as the greatest disaster, likely to have flooded upwards of 3,000 square miles and displace some 50,000 inhabitants. Built jointly by the state and the federal government at a cost of $250,000, with a 200-foot base and up to 30 feet high, the Morganza levee was considered one of the finest on the Mississippi and protected a large portion of south Louisiana, including thousands of acres of the all-important sugarcane fields. Besides worrying about crop damage in the millions of dollars, local officials were telegraphing the governor to send rescue boats "as otherwise there will be a heavy loss of life."

Toward the end of June 1892, newspaper accounts described another flooding:

> On last Sunday morning at 8 o'clock the levee which protected the town of Bayou Sara, on the Bayou side, gave way and in a few hours the town was under an average of 10 feet of water. Very fortunately, the occurrence had been expected and most of the residents had removed families, horses, cattle and chickens to places of safety on the neighboring hill. For several days previous to the break the water had risen higher than the small levee and was held out altogether by means of sacks of earth. The loss of property is considerable.

A levee break was also reported at this time at Angola, then the plantation of Major S. L. James before the state purchased that property and adjoining lands for use as the state penitentiary.

In October 1892, it was reported that "the citizens of St. Francisville and Bayou Sara are determined to rebuild their dismantled levee and to do it with their own funds and in such a manner as to secure for ever and age to the little town at the foot of the hill immunity from the river's ravages." Of course that was not to be, as the struggle would be on-going, but there were printed accounts of concerts and dramatic performances staged as fundraisers for the levee fund in Bayou Sara. In late October newspapers reported "the first installment of laborers, stock and utensils for the building of the Bayou Sara levee were sent over from New Texas by Mr. Morgan O'Connel, the contractor." By December the optimistic reports in the *Feliciana Sentinel* said "The Bayou Sara levee is rapidly nearing completion.... Judging from the dimensions of the work already finished we would say, no more overflow for Bayou Sara."

High water on the river sometimes also disrupted railroad service and mail delivery, as reported in 1897: "Owing to a considerable portion of the

The steam-powered sternwheeler *William Edenborne* transports a train across the Mississippi River. Courtesy of the West Feliciana Historical Society.

railroad tract between Bayou Sara and Slaughter being under water, our mail facilities have been lessened. Instead of getting our mail from that source at 5 o'clock in the evening, we now get it at 7 o'clock on the *Cleon* from Baton Rouge. This will only be until the water goes down."

Even in the midst of the constant flooding, there could be occasional levity, as related by Mary Alice Lambert in an article for the Baton Rouge *Morning Advocate* (1952). A certain Captain Mossop and his family were living in the Methodist Parsonage in Bayou Sara when a break in the levee flooded the town in 1897. Moving to the more substantial Methodist Church, they took with them all their household furnishings along with their chickens, cats, and dogs, with Mrs. Mossop and her daughter occupying one side of the second-floor interior balcony and the dogs, cats, and chickens installed on the other side. Captain Mossop elected to sleep on springs and mattress atop the pews below, a decision he no doubt regretted when the water rose more than a foot an hour and was twelve feet deep in the church. Mrs. Lambert said, "The only known casualties were the chickens that dropped off their high perches and were drowned in the water below. The family lived in the church for a month."

Beulah Smith Watts, of Solitude Plantation along the banks of Bayou Sara creek just above the port, wrote vividly of the flood of 1912:

The 1906 flood of Bayou Sara, with horses and buggies, raised walkways connecting shops, pirogues, exuberant little boys, and waterfowl in the streets. Courtesy of the West Feliciana Historical Society.

The aftermath of the flood could be devastating for residents and businesses alike. Courtesy of the West Feliciana Historical Society.

A flat-bottom skiff loaded with supplies, perhaps being salvaged from a flooded store or being transported to flood victims elsewhere. Courtesy of the West Feliciana Historical Society.

The rainy season began in the early spring of 1912. The melting ice and snow from the north began to swell the river. The Mississippi River began to rise and flood the low land. The levee which protected the town became threatened. Rains and winds caused alarm. The citizens of Bayou Sara worked day and night in the rain, filling sand bags to bank the levee in weakening places. School boys worked with them. Sand boils began to appear. Citizens of Bayou Sara were ordered to move livestock and possessions to higher lands. The rains had stopped, but the winds were high. ... The school was in St. Francisville. On May 2, 1912, before classes had started, whistles began blowing, and bells began tolling. We knew what had happened! School was dismissed, and we pupils ran to Catholic Hill to see the water rushing in, swallowing the town of Bayou Sara. The roar of onrushing water could be heard for miles. The crevasse was 187 feet wide. The next day nothing but the tops of houses was visible. Most of the houses were swept away by the strong current of rushing water, and debris floated in the water.

Some of the rich merchants moved away; others rolled structures up the hill to safety in St. Francisville or salvaged what lumber was usable and rebuilt on the bluff. Deserted buildings fell into decay and, according to Mrs. Watts, only a couple of brick buildings and the railroad station remained.

The May 4, 1912, edition of the *Dunkirk* (New York) *Evening Observer* was headlined "Southern Cities Are Being Flooded: Streets of Bayou Sara in Louisiana Are Under 25 Feet of Water—Crest Reaches Baton Rouge." Postmarked New Orleans, the article described how gangs of workmen are today battling with the waters of the Mississippi to prevent the flooding of Baton Rouge. With the town of Bayou Sara, only twenty miles north of the capital practically swept away and the levees about the capital threatening to go out at any minute, the situation in this state today was extremely serious. The people of Melville have fled from their homes, while portions of New Orleans itself are threatened. The water is nearly a foot higher than at any time in the history of the city. Workmen are guarding the levees at the foot of Canal street, the chief business thoroughfare where the waters are lapping the top of the dikes.

Continuing under the heading "People Taken From Homes," the dispatch said:

On orders of Captain Logan of the army flood relief corps the people of Melville were taken from their homes late yesterday. Two special trains were rushed to the scene. The women and children were first taken from the town. At night one train returned and the men, who stayed behind to continue the fight against the waters, were taken out. At Bayou Sara, today the streets are under 25 feet of water. When the waters rushed in late yesterday, houses were toppled from their foundations. A great sheet of water leaping through a gap in the levee 300 feet wide swept everything before it. The smaller buildings were dashed against the more substantial

The view of Bayou Sara looking down the hill from St. Francisville, which was high enough to be safe from the floodwaters. Courtesy of the West Feliciana Historical Society.

structures and the debris carried on by the flood. There was scant warning of the break in the levee, and panic reined for a time.

Left All Belongings Behind: Men and women ran wildly into their homes, picked up their children and fled, leaving all their belongings behind. Others took their positions in boats, and were picked up by the crest of the flood, and carried miles from the town. Couriers rode through the country districts spreading the alarm. The farmers, driving their livestock before them, headed for high ground as rapidly as possible. Today additional hundreds are homeless or without food or shelter. The government rescue corps are overwhelmed with the task before them, but small boats are being sent out as rapidly as possible to bring in the refugees, many of whom are marooned in tops of trees.

The area suffered an additional loss when its Congressman, Robert C. Wickliffe, who had worked tirelessly to secure financial aid for the flooded districts, especially the stricken town of Bayou Sara, was run down and killed by a southbound Southern Railway train at Washington on an embankment near the Potomac River railroad bridge where he had intended to go fishing.

And as bad as the flood of 1912 was, it paled in comparison to the deluges of the 1920s, especially the great flood of April 1927 that displaced close to a million people along the Mississippi River corridor, causing thousands of deaths and threatening millions of acres of land. It was one of the world's most devastating floods, called "the last uncontrolled rampage of the Mississippi River." As months of heavy rains upriver overflowed all of the tributaries, the Mississippi River exceeded the highest flood marks ever, carrying an astounding flow of more than three million cubic feet of water every second above Bayou Sara in Greenville, Mississippi, according to John M. Barry's exceptional book, *Rising Tide*. Barry notes that along the Lower Mississippi

the flood put as much as thirty feet of water over lands where 931,159 people . . . had lived. Twenty-seven thousand square miles were inundated. . . . As late as July 1, 1.5 million acres remained underwater. . . . An estimated 330,000 people were rescued from rooftops, trees, isolated patches of high ground, and levees. The Red Cross ran 154 "concentration camps," tent cities, in seven states. . . . A total of 325,554 people, the majority of them African-Americans, lived in these camps for as long as four months. An additional 311,922 people outside the camps were fed and clothed by the Red Cross.

After that one, the Corps of Engineers got serious about construction of substantial levee systems and constructed the Old River Control Structure and Morganza floodway to divert Mississippi floodwaters into the Atchafalaya River and the Bonnet Carre spillway to divert even more of the Mississippi's overflow into Lake Pontchartrain. These were intended to at least protect the heavily populated urban areas like Baton Rouge and New Orleans to the south.

They came way too late to save the little port city of Bayou Sara.

7

Wartime Memoirs

Records of life in early Bayou Sara can be found in a number of sources, such as census and death records, merchant account books, newspaper dispatches, print advertisements for businesses, and family genealogies; but the most interesting of all are the personal journals.

W. G. Schafer's records begin with his landing in Bayou Sara on a flatboat on January 22, 1855, after having been in transit from Cincinnati since the beginning of November 1854. He records his experiences beginning as a clerk for merchants Whiteman and Hatch at a salary of $20 a month. By 1857, having received salary raises to $25 and then $30 monthly, he had prospered sufficiently to establish his own business on a flatboat, travelling to New Orleans to purchase his stock and opening for business in March. In July he married Augusta Oehlman from Bremen, Germany.

The couple seems to have lived on the flatboat, from which they sold moss and other items—on July 23 he records receiving a bill of sale for $144.50 for moss he'd shipped in January to Ohio. From his journals, Mr. Schafer seems a man of few words and little emotion; sowing a bed of turnips, weaning himself off cigar smoking, his cow calving, and attending a Jewish circumcision get as much attention in his memoir as the birth and death of his own children. His commercial efforts, however, get a lot more space, shedding light on the struggles to carry on businesses in Bayou Sara amidst the Civil War.

In 1858 there were troubles galore, as recorded:

May 10: I removed my Boat up to the foot of the Hill on acct. of high water.

May 17: I removed my boat back to the flatboat landing at B. Sara.

July 14: My wife was accidently shot in the head.

Oct. 1: My brother-in-law, Dr. Chs. Oehlman left here this day for Evansville, Ind.

Wait! Mrs. Schafer shot in the head? Did she live? Did she die? Did he shoot her? Did someone else shoot her? But alas, we have no more detail from the journaler, who considered it worth only a scant mention along with his business accountings. Apparently, she did survive the shooting, as in 1860 he records their trip north by railroad and steamboat, visiting his brother in New York where his Louisiana money was refused by the proprietor of a store on Broadway. And this:

> January 27, 1861: My wife gave birth (on Sunday) to a pair of twins 9 A.M. Boy & Girl.

Other postings from 1860-61, during which time Schafer apparently was able to continue his commercial activities in spite of having joined the West Feliciana Rifles, describe floods and fires, boats breaking loose after storms and high water, illnesses like Dengue fever, and purchasing properties.

The war is mentioned in these early years only in passing:

> May 11: This day the West Feliciana Rifle Company was presented with a Silk Flag by our Town Ladies—Speeches were made by Miss Doherty, Mr. Dawson Austin & a Boy named Eugene DeViney.

> May 12: This day I went out to the Soldiers Camp with my wife and my Son Frank.

> July 25: Capt. R.H. Barrow's Company left this day for Virginia.

> Nov. 16: Capt. W.W. Leake's Cavalry Company went on Board the *Magnolia* for Kentucky.

And still, life went on, including enjoyable entertainments:

> March 21, 1861: Went with my wife to Harry McCartha's Show/Concert.

> March 23: I went again by myself.

> April 15: I partook of a Party given by Mr. C.J.Wolflin at his residence yesterday—his birthday.

> Oct. 2: Sowed 2 Beds Turnips this Evening.

> Nov. 9: Quit smoking cigars.

April 23, 1862: This day I smoked the first Cigar since December 9/61.

There were hardships and scarcities, as itemized in this entry:

May 29: Flour per Bbl (hardly to be had)....................$40.00
Bacon or Pork none.
Coffee sold 8/ none now.
Lard per lb (very scarce)...................50
Candles none in Stores
Liquors none for sale
Cigars very scarce none but home manufacture at 5 cents per piece
Supplies from New Orleans are entirely cut off.

In August of 1862 he records being "arrested by a party of Federals off the *Essex* on suspicion of being a Soldier or a Conscript in the Confederate Service." After being released, he returned to Bayou Sara and managed to move his family to a safer location before being assigned to picket duty as the *Essex* returned to the area and began shelling, then landed a party of about twenty troops who "commenced setting the town of Bayou Sara on fire. The whole front extending two squares back was destroyed by night." By September 1862, after sporadic engagements and retaliations, he records that a total of sixty-seven structures were destroyed by the *Essex*, including the WFRR Depot, the sawmill, Hampton Witaker's hotel, the livery stables, the printing office, and a number of other businesses and homes.

The *Essex*, to which Shafer refers in the above posting, was a steam-powered ferryboat modified for use in the Civil War with iron armor, turning it into a one-thousand-ton river gunboat used by both the U.S. Army and U.S. Navy. Commanding officer Commodore William David Porter had his ship completely re-engineered, lengthened, widened, and equipped with more powerful engines and armor, after which the *Essex* took part in operations near Vicksburg in the summer of 1862, then joined Admiral David Farragut's squadron as the only Federal ironclad on the Lower Mississippi.

In August of 1862 the *Essex* helped repel a Confederate attack on Baton Rouge, and then, according to an article by C.E. Lester in *Harper's New Monthly Magazine*, she steamed upriver to procure coal at Bayou Sara, arriving there on the 10th.

The presence of the *Essex* caused some commotion among the inhabitants, as considerable supplies of subsistence stores, just brought across

USS Essex, ca.1862. The *Essex*, a steam-powered ferryboat modified for use in the Civil War and commanded by U.S. Navy Commodore William D. Porter, shelled and burned much of Bayou Sara in 1862. Courtesy of the 'Andrew D. Lytle's Baton Rouge' Photograph Collection, Louisiana and Lower Mississippi Valley Collections, LSU Libraries, Baton Rouge, La.

the river from West Louisiana, were on the levee awaiting transportation to the Confederate forces in the interior under Generals Ruggles and Breckinridge. This town is a terminus of a railroad running from the State of Mississippi and Northeastern Louisiana, and prior to the war carried on a very important trade with the interior.

The mayor of Bayou Sara was summoned on board for a meeting with Commander Porter, who guaranteed the safety of inhabitants and respect for personal property "as long as there was reciprocity toward Federals observed" and that the coal laying at the wharf be supplied to the *Essex* as contraband of war rather than private property. Any Federal prisoners being held by municipal authorities were also to be delivered to the gunboat.

The U.S. steam-ram *Sumter* was left anchored off the town of Bayou Sara to protect the captured stores as the *Essex* returned to Baton Rouge. The protection was considered necessary because, as the article states,

> there were indications of desire on the part of the municipal authorities to break the amicable arrangement made with the Mayor. Threats against the lives of Union men had been made. . . . Considerable excitement

existed at this time among the inhabitants of towns on the Lower Mississippi, in consequence of outrages constantly being committed by the troops in occupation of Baton Rouge on the Confederate population.

U.S. Naval records refer to the town of St. Francisville as "a perfect hotbed of secession . . . the constant resort of Confederates."

The gunboat *Sumter* unfortunately grounded itself and was abandoned by her crew in fear of attack. The *Essex* rushed back to Bayou Sara on August 23 but found the *Sumter* destroyed and Union sympathizers maltreated or shot at. The stores the *Sumter* was to have guarded were also destroyed and much of the coal burned. When forces from the *Essex* advanced into the town, they came under heavy musket fire, and the ship's guns returned fire. Consequently, to avoid repetition of attack, all houses along the levee were burned by Union forces to prevent their being used as cover by the enemy. On the 29th, when an armed crew from the *Essex* attempted to recover what coal was left at Bayou Sara, guerillas launched an attack on them from the markethouse and remaining buildings. The attack was returned, the guerillas driven out, and Union troops burned the markethouse and what buildings were left in what they called "this treacherous town."

One contemporary account was quoted by Robert M. Browning Jr. in his book *Lincoln's Trident: The West Gulf Blockading Squadron During the Civil War*, as saying that the *Essex* "laid the town in ruins," leaving only a few frame buildings and the walls of some brick structures, so that the remains looked like "some ancient castles in the old world." He surmised that Porter's August 10 shelling of the wharf area of Bayou Sara and compelling local slaves to load 450 hogsheads of sugar onto the transport probably resulted in the guerilla attack on the crew Porter sent ashore on the 23rd, saying the local militia commander was unsure if the Union forces meant to stay or "have merely come on a thieving errand."

Shafer continued to record his daily struggles. In spite of periodic illnesses: (Sept. 28, 1862: Took chills and fever but cured it in a few days with Calomel & Bitters cooked from Cherry Root, Dogwood and Poplar Bark") he attempted to continue in commerce—and what a struggle it did entail. Having entered into co-partnership with S. Felson, the two merchants made a laborious trip downriver to acquire stock:

Oct. 11: Went to town and started with Felson for Plaquemines. We stopped at Port Hudson, had our papers approved, crossed the River and in front of Lobdell's Store for tonight.

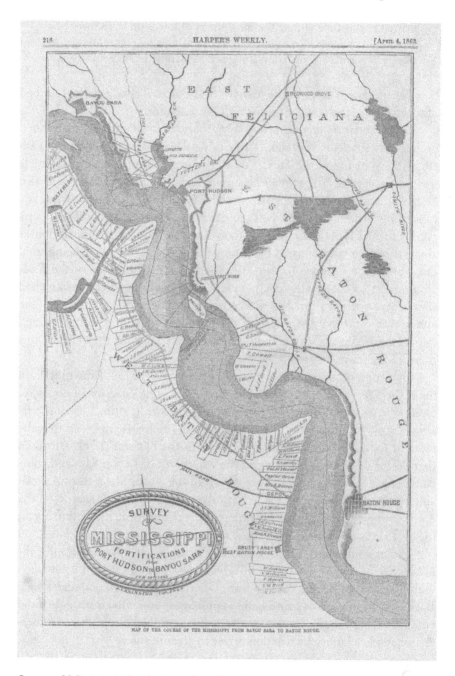

Survey of Mississippi fortifications from Port Hudson to Bayou Sara: Feb. 10th 1863.
Courtesy of the University of Texas at Arlington Library.

Oct. 12: 3 A.M. Started and arrived in Plaquemine at 12 M.

Oct. 13: Made purchases of Dry Goods & Rum.

Oct. 14: Put our goods on a Wagon and started for Home 9 A.M. Camped at Lobdell's Store this night.

Oct. 15: Arrived opposite Port Hudson 8 A.M. Felson went on in the Buggy and I waited until 3 P.M. for the Rum, which we had shipped on a Mule Team from Lobdell's Store. I took Rum on our hired Wagon, started and came to Waterloo at night, where I stored the Rum and went on with Dry Goods. I stopped at Flechieux's Hotel for the night.

Oct. 16: Hired a cart from John Bemis and had Rum hauled to the ferry, crossed the River with all and got everything in the Store by 4 P.M. and went home after that.

Oct. 17: We exchanged most of the Goods for Tobacco.

The following months brought heartache.

Nov. 14, 1962: My wife was delivered of a dead boy under severe pains 3 A.M.

Nov. 15: Buried child 10 A.M.

Jan. 25, 1863: My son Charley took sick and I send for Dr. Whicher.

Jan. 31: Charley died from the effects of sore throat 5 P.M.

Feb. 1: Charley was buried 5 P.M.

And still Schafer dispassionately described life in Bayou Sara as a mixture of continuing commerce and war.

May 7: Bought lot of F. McCarney $200.00.

May 21: Dissolved Partnership with Mr. Mann.

May 22: Late at night the federals under General Banks made their landing here for the attack upon Port Hudson.

May 24: The fight of Port Hudson commenced. Troops are landing here continuously coming by Boats from Simmesport.

May 25: Mr. Mann was robbed last night the second time by Federal stragglers. I received Mr. Mann and family with movables in my house.

May 29: Seven Conf. Soldiers came to Town on horseback 4 of whom fired upon a party of Federal soldiers among which was Cpt. Johnson all in a yawl near the House of Mrs. Turner. S.M. Leake living there at the time. Steamers *Jackson* and *Australia* fired a few Shells after that party towards the Hills and they escaped unhurt.

June 30: The gunboats being under the impression that Conf. soldiers were in St. Francisville, fired about 35 shells towards that town. Several houses damaged but nobody hurt.

July 1: A party of Frierson's Cavalry made their appearance in St. Francisville and it was believed that they had Orders to burn that town . . . people were in great distress. Nothing happened. The cavalry left.

July 8: Gun boats and Transports lying here received Orders to sail down Stream at 2 P.M.

July 10: Bought Mr. Mann's Bay horse for $100.00.

And into 1864 the same mix of business, floods, health woes, and war continued unabated. Schafer dispassionately records the daily events as Bayou Sara's residents suffered incursions from both sides of the battle:

Jan. 4: Went with Goods on *Mittie Stephens* 5 P.M.

Jan. 9: Freeman and J. Mann were arrested by a USS party of fifty Confederates. Freeman returned but Mann was taken to Camp. Cpt. J.P. Foster, Comd. *USS Lafayette*, demanded of Col. Adams the release of J. Mann. It was refused and Foster in retaliation after having given 48 hours notice fired 107 Shells into St. Francisville and thereby damaging a good many Houses (done from 1 ½ P.M. to 4 P.M. 10th inst.)

Jan. 10: 3 A.M. 4 Wagons with 3 light cannons and Conf. escort came to town and took all of Mr. D.T. Riley's Stores, some of R.M. Leake's, searched Mrs. Gauchee's and Maguire's Houses and went out.

Jan. 17: 4 P.M. 26 Bales of Cotton were burnt at the landing opposite the *Lafayette*. The *Lafayette* fired two Shells.

Jan. 19: 8 P.M. A party of 33 Conf. Soldiers appeared in town burnt 5 Bales of Cotton, took two Mules from A. Trice, arrested M. Riley and Henderson, took $3540.00 from H and let him go but kept M. Riley after taken his money about $510.00, took him to Camp. They also took some Dry Goods from Mrs. Barton at her House. A shell was fired by the *Lafayette* and the soldiers left town.

Feb. 3: got sick and employed Dr. Engle. Had the bilious colic, layed in bed six weeks after which I got up and gaining strength slowly and went on Board of a Steamboat for N. Orleans.

Life continued, as did death.

Oct. 22, 1865: 6 P.M. A pair of twins, Boy and Girl. Boy dead. Girl in good health. Buried Boy October 3, 4 P.M.

April 9, 1866: Having had several heavy rains for the last ten days, made it impossible to pass along the streets in town dry footed as the rainwater had no chance of running off on a/c of the river being very high.

Oct. 20, 1866: R.M. Leake was killed by M. Reynolds.

Nov. 22: My wife and I attended a Jewish Circumsizing.

Nov. 25: My son Frank gave his friends a party this day in honor of his 7th Birthday, which was on the 23rd int.

Feb. 16, 1867: At the election occasioned by vacancy I was elected Alderman of Bayou Sara this day by 16 votes.

Feb. 22, 1868: Locked pipe and Tobacco up 4 P.M.

April 1: Portrait Painter (Woodford Sanders) took possession of one Room of House Lot 234.

April 9: G. Miller (tailor) took possession of half of house 234 at $9 per month.

May 1: Saw Negro man hung named Edmond Harrison.

May 9: Planted Irish Potatoes in my garden.

May 31: My cow calfed 7 P.M.

July 17: Bottled off Keg of Catawba Wine (Present for Chs. Ohlmann), 54 bottles-1 broke 2 drank leaves 51.

August 19: Shipped 7 Bales of Moss with 7 belonging to C.J. Wolflin on *Milgour* to Evansville (My weight 2127, CJW's 2484).

And then in the winter of 1868, after having received an offer from Rudolph F. Theurer to enter into business with him, Mr. Schafer sold his business and real estate holdings and left Bayou Sara with his family for New Orleans.

8

The Day the War Stopped

In June 1863, some ten miles south of Bayou Sara overland, the bloody Siege of Port Hudson pitted 30,000 Union troops under Major General Nathaniel P. Banks against 6,800 weary Confederates under Major General Franklin Gardner, as they fought over the all-important control of traffic on the Mississippi River. Port Hudson and Vicksburg were the only rebel strongholds left along the Mississippi, and if the Union forces could wrest from them control of the river traffic, they could cut off supplies from the west and completely separate one-third of the Confederacy.

Considered the most important Confederate fortification on the Lower Mississippi, with heavy batteries commanding the narrowest point in the river below St. Louis, Port Hudson's location was at the terminus of the Clinton & Port Hudson Railroad. It was a little town of some three hundred inhabitants atop the White Cliffs from which large amounts of cotton and sugar were shipped.

Admiral David Farragut had attempted to destroy Confederate cannons atop the bluffs from the river, but of his seven ships, four were turned back, one was completely destroyed, and only his flagship and the USS *Albatross* passed upriver from Port Hudson safely, leaving ground troops to fight it out for nearly another month.

The *Albatross* was patrolling the Mississippi River off the port city of Bayou Sara just below St. Francisville when a single shot rang out from the captain's stateroom. It was 4:15 p.m. on June 11, and the vessel's commander, John Elliot Hart of Schenectady, New York, lay mortally wounded on the floor, his pistol beside his body and a note detailing his despondency over his sufferings from dyspepsia. Attempts to find a metal coffin in which to ship his body home proved futile, and so the ship's surgeon went ashore in hopes of making arrangements for burial on land.

The ship's surgeon was a Mason; Commander Hart was also a Mason. Living near the river he found several helpful brothers named White who were also Masons; Samuel White owned the Bayou Sara ferry, and Benjamin White was owner of the steamboat *Red Chief,* operating on the

U.S. Navy gunboat *Albatross* ca. 1861-65. In 1863 the gunboat *USS Albatross* was one of only two federal vessels to make it past the Confederate blockade on the Mississippi River at Port Hudson, setting the stage for a most unusual ceasefire. Courtesy of the 'Andrew D. Lytle's Baton Rouge' Photograph Collection, Louisiana and Lower Mississippi Valley Collections, LSU Libraries, Baton Rouge, La.

Red River. And in St. Francisville was Feliciana Lodge No. 31 F&AM, the second oldest Masonic Lodge in the state. Its senior warden, William Walter Leake, was a Confederate cavalry officer who happened to be at home on furlough to visit his wife Margaret, daughter of Capt. Robinson Mumford, banker of Bayou Sara. It would be his duty, this Confederate officer felt, to afford a decent burial to a fellow Mason and fellow military officer, regardless of politics. And so the war stopped, if only for a few mournful moments, and Commander Hart was laid to rest in the cemetery around Grace Episcopal Church, with Union and Confederate Masons participating in the burial services along with the Episcopal rector, the Reverend Daniel Lewis.

An article in the New Orleans *Times-Picayune* in 1937 called this event "one of the strangest born of the War Between the States, when fighting men could battle to the death and yet know chivalry, when war had not become the cold-blooded butchery of today." Hart's death was announced rather insensitively in his hometown paper, the Schenectady *Democrat and Reflector*, on June 25, 1863, by a New Orleans correspondent of the New York *Herald*, as follows:

> I regret to announce that I have this moment learned from a gentleman who arrived from the river this afternoon that Lieutenant Commander John E. Hart, United States Navy, Commander of the gunboat *Albatross*, committed suicide night before last by blowing his brains out with a

pistol. He had been ill for a few days past with fever, and it is supposed to have affected his brain in a manner to render him insane. He is thought to have been in that condition when the act was committed. Lieutenant Commander Hart was an officer highly esteemed and beloved in the service. . . . He leaves a wife and family in New York to whom his loss will be irreparable. They have the sympathy of all in their sore affliction.

This unusual event is celebrated each year in June in St. Francisville, with Civil War re-enactors in blue and gray participating—some actual descendants of the original participants and others coming down from Hart's Schenectady, New York, Masonic lodge to join the festivities. Vintage dancers, period music, drama, history talks, lodge tours, and the re-created burial are all part of this unique program. Preserving a moment of civility in the midst of a bloody war, this is a re-enactment that celebrates not a battle but the bonds of brotherhood that proved stronger even than the divisiveness of a bitter civil conflict. They call it "The Day the War Stopped," and that is exactly what happened—at least for a little while.

∽

The merchants of Bayou Sara struggled to continue their commercial ventures during and after the Civil War, but it was certainly a struggle. Just before the war began, a raging fire had destroyed nearly all of the structures in the center of town, and residents were just rebuilding when the Civil War brought major damage as men, produce, and war materials moved through the little port city. Life was totally disrupted, and not just for the outlying cotton plantation owners and slaves who worked their fields. Once the all-important cotton production faltered, repercussions were felt all along the credit chain, from planter to merchant, from factor to mill.

During the war years, some planters tried to hold back cotton harvests in hopes of better market conditions later. Blockades and trade prohibitions kept other cotton off the market. Black market trade sprang up, with southern cotton being slipped across the border in Texas to be sold through Mexico and shipped to England from there. But many planters left their fields to answer the Confederacy's call to arms, and many of the slaves who picked the crop fled, so much of the cotton harvest either went unpicked or was destroyed by Union troops. By the time the war was over and a new labor force of sharecroppers (often former slaves) was in place, the reign of King Cotton was over. Prices fluctuated, bad weather caused crop failures, the boll weevil decimated crops, and land was depleted from over-reliance on one-crop agriculture. The cotton planters had little or no

Confederate Masons joined Union naval officers to stop the war, if only for a moment, to provide a dignified burial for Union gunboat commander John E. Hart in the cemetery surrounding Grace Episcopal Church, as seen in the re-enactment of his 1863 interment beneath moss-covered live oaks. Photos courtesy of Darrell Chitty.

money, even less credit, and it would be to the Jewish merchants that they would turn for help.

For a picture of life in the Felicianas around Bayou Sara in the months right after the war ended, the New Orleans *Times-Picayune* of September 19, 1865, provides a telling description:

> A short visit up the coast as far as Bayou Sara, and into the interior of West Feliciana, afforded us an opportunity of observing the condition of affairs in that region; the prospects of crops, etc., which, though hurried and superficial, was not uninstructive nor as discouraging as we apprehended. It is true there is much uncertainty and apprehension as to the future among the planters and among the negroes, who, though generally peaceful and orderly, are unsettled and careless as to the present. All the evils we could observe in the state of the industry and cultivation of the country are due to the want of proper regulations, which will assure the negroes full protection, stated employment, judicious compensation, and the planters the certainty of labor to cultivate and gather their crops. Without some satisfactory and efficient regulations on these subjects the negroes will abandon the planters, or the planters will abandon them.
>
> In the Felicianas, where there is a very large negro population—West Feliciana alone having four negroes to one white man—the planters have been compelled, in many cases, to discharge and send off from the plantations large numbers of negroes from sheer inability to support them. On very few of the plantations are the negroes paid. They are generally willing to stay at their old homes for their food and clothing, but unless good crops are made the planters cannot even afford this expense. Good crops, even very moderate crops, cannot be made unless by a larger amount of labor than the negroes are generally willing to render in their present unsettled condition. In their ignorance, they are constantly expecting some change which will vastly improve their circumstances. "Roast beef and two dollars a day," city life, are constantly disturbing their imagination and tempting them to indolence and indifference to the future. The planters are reluctant to lose their old laborers, and many make the sacrifices to retain them; but the bad crops of this season will not enable them to support the large forces which used to find abundant employment in gathering cotton.
>
> Even corn, of which large crops were planted, will be very short this season owing to long drought, followed by heavy rains. The sweet potato crop, a large means of subsistence in this region, has been seriously damaged by the same causes. As for the cotton, it may be as great a failure as last year, when the worm devastated the whole country. The drought caused

the bolls to rot and the heavy winds and rains have beaten them to the ground. There can be no exaggeration in the accounts of the unpromising condition of this crop. The parish of West Feliciana, whose ordinary crop in old times used to be some fifteen or twenty thousand bales, will not this season produce eight hundred bales. . . .

Despite all these unpromising symptoms and condition of affairs in this region, that which encouraged and consoled us was the general cheerfulness, hopefulness, patience and industry of the people. There seemed to be no disposition to repine or despair, no morose discontent and querulousness. Everybody appeared to be doing their best to repair the terrible damages of the war, to restore order and accommodate themselves to the changed condition of affairs. This spirit is especially observable among the returned Confederate soldiers, who may be seen everywhere, with their coats off, hard at work, putting their hands to every kind of honest labor. It is this spirit which will bring this country and this people out of the present troubles. The old stay-at-homes are very despondent and complaining, and grumble exceedingly over the present discomforts, but the young soldiers, who have suffered extreme hardships, adapt themselves gracefully and easily to the demands of the times, accept the situation, and put their hands to any employment by which they may obtain an honest livelihood.

Of course there were many young soldiers, and old ones too, who never returned from the war, and many who did return were disabled, debilitated, or despondent, despite the optimism of the *Times-Picayune* reporter who visited Bayou Sara and the Felicianas shortly after the close of the war. As the planters and the slaves and the cash crops went, so went the merchants of Bayou Sara; times would never be flush again.

9

Reconstruction

Having made it through the Civil War (barely) and recurring natural disasters, the Bayou Sara/St. Francisville area struggled to survive the aftermath of war. Louisiana politics, always known for amusing shenanigans and sometimes downright dishonesty, took a violent turn for the worse during Reconstruction. Bayou Sara's Julius Freyhan was caught right in the middle of one bizarre episode in 1874. A newspaper dispatch in September 1874 was headed: "The Disturbance in West Feliciana: Machinations of an Ambitious German Carpet-bagger—A Terror in a Political Dodge— Failure of the Scheme."

The article described Bayou Sara as

the remnant of a once flourishing town on the Mississippi, some few miles above Baton Rouge. It was burned by Admiral Porter during the war. After that affair, although Bayou Sara was too good a business point to be abandoned, yet the great majority of the inhabitants removed their homes to St. Francisville, a village on the heights about one mile east of the river. The stores, the magazines, etc. remained at Bayou Sara, which still serves as the *entrepot* for the surrounding country for forty miles back, until one strikes the line of the railroad from Memphis to New Orleans. It receives from the steamboats all the corn, bacon, etc. needed by the population, which, raising nothing but cotton, cannot well feed itself. And it is the depot for the cotton which should pay largely for the devotion of its cultivators, but which does not. The population of the parish, which it will be remembered is the same thing as a county in other states, gives a large Negro majority, but in both Bayou Sara and St. Francisville the whites are in the majority, though not largely.

The article goes on to describe the politics of the region. The governor and his faction apparently kept strong control over all the political appointments, filling the offices with "conservatives" of both races. "So long as the machinery of voting and the assessment and collection of taxes were in the right hands, i.e. in hands devoted to himself, the governor was never averse to conciliating the country by appointing mayors and parish attorneys and others, even though they were of the opposite political stripe."

And so it happened that in Bayou Sara, the mayor, police justice, and parish attorney were all conservative appointees of Governor Kellogg; as was the sheriff, a conservative black man and an industrious, hard-working carpenter who had been made postmaster by Kellogg and later sheriff through "a little conspiracy of Emile Weber, a German carpet-bagger, a state senator and leader of the colored element in the parish. Weber had distributed the principal offices among his own relatives and wanted the post office . . . in the interest of his mother, who kept a general store and whose business, it was thought, would be increased thereby." When Weber asked the postmaster to resign and accept a state office, he refused, so Weber procured an appointment for him as sheriff, thinking he would then have to give up the post office position. But because of the low salary for the post, the statutes did not prevent the sheriff from holding county office as well; and so the black postmaster also became sheriff, and the German carpetbagger declared war.

Another gentleman had also noticed "the disposition of Mr. Weber to grab all the offices for himself and friends." John Gair of Pointe Coupee Parish wanted to run for state senate but was opposed by Weber. Weber obtained the nomination of John Breaux, a conservative white man, to oppose Gair, who was black and smart enough to put on his slate the sheriff of West Feliciana, another very popular and well-respected African American candidate. Weber feared the Gair ticket would split the black vote, and so he determined to ignite the flames of fear and passion in the electorate.

On the night of Wednesday, September 16, 1874, the mayor of Bayou Sara, Mr. Irvine,

> was awakened by a German messenger from the store of a Jewish merchant, a Mr. Freyhan, who has several stores in St. Francisville and one notably on the outskirts of the village, where the Jackson and Woodville roads meet together. The man bore a note from the merchant which bade Mr. Irvine to ready to receive a body of armed and mounted Negroes, who were determined to sack and burn the town. The information had been given by a colored clergyman, a Mr. George Dent, who declared that during two meetings in the woods, when this thing had been discussed, he had endeavored to fight it down. But his counsels had been overruled, and the outrage was determined on.

An alarmed Mayor Irvine immediately dressed and rushed to consult with the parish attorney, Mr. Leake. Agreeing that the thing was "only too likely," they enlisted the aid of the sheriff, who called out and armed a posse, put himself at their head, and patrolled all night until 4 a.m., seeing and hearing nothing.

The following day, it was discovered that Mr. Weber had telegraphed for troops, saying the whites were up in arms and a reign of terror was imminent, and that he feared for his life. The others felt Freyhan had been "humbugged" and there was no movement toward riot by the African American populace at all. But shortly thereafter, a black man raced into town breathless to announce hundreds of "mounted, armed Negroes in the field intent on mischief." When a scout confirmed the alarm as true this time, the sheriff again called out a posse, including "five colored men, who own property in the place and were not going to have any foolery about their homes," and sent for assistance from neighboring parishes as well.

Posting some armed guards around the courthouse, the sheriff led the rest of the posse to positions behind a fence to meet a body of men coming down the Woodville road. The newspaper accounts report the exchange of challenges in a manner that would surely not pass an editor's sense of propriety or political correctness today, saying that as the rioters streamed down the Woodville road, they were "challenged by a voice from the fence, 'Who comes there?' but the exceedingly unmilitary reply was returned, 'Who de debbil's dat?' Again rang out the challenge, 'Who comes there?' and again the response was evasive, 'Who's you?'" Shots rang out from the advancing invaders, answered by a volley from the sheriff's posse. After five minutes of firing, the invaders broke ranks and ran.

The newspaper account reports no injuries. "It will seem incredible to the fair sex," the article reported, "who generally believe that some one's life is in danger if an unloaded gun be only in the room, but it is a fact that in all that firing no one was hit on either side. The colored men were badly scared, however, for they left behind them one horse, one mule, two shotguns, three pistols and four old hats. This was the battle."

As day broke the next morning, it was discovered that the band that had been defeated

> had broken into Freyhan's further store before they advanced, and had with threats demanded ammunition. The powder had been hidden in anticipation of trouble, but they took all the buckshot and helped themselves to tobacco, and to a filthy poisonous liquid called anisette, of which they are very fond. Some began to plunder promiscuously, but the

leaders tore the things out of their hands and pushed them away from the shelves and counters. Some were very peaceable indeed, and insisted on paying for their tobacco and drink. But there were some who demanded kerosene and kindling-wood, that they might burn the town.

They went into another store, also at the outskirts, for this, but close by lived a colored woman who owned that building, and she came to defend her property, and pushed them out, the cowardly German proprietor who rented the place from her having fled in abject terror. He actually, it appeared afterward, forced himself into a thorn hedge—the Cherokee rose, which grows very thick and high—leaving his store to the mercy of the assailants. But the old lady was so fierce and reproachful that she drove them off. It may appear strange to the readers of *The Times* that these stores should be outside of the town, but the business done is entirely with the country Negroes, who bring their cotton and products for barter. It is therefore a better locality than within the precincts of the town.

The ploy by Weber to start a race riot failed, and his opponent Mr. Gair profited by his failed shenanigans. Gair took advantage of the situation by changing his slate to half conservative white candidates and half blacks. Said the newspaper account, "The plundering and stealing of the Weber party have disgusted all the intelligent colored men. It is notorious that the school teachers have not been paid for a long time, and that the Police Jury have divided the money. They have run the parish in debt $10,000 in a few years, without anything to show for it."

Across the river from Bayou Sara, the Weber faction tried similar methods of inciting racial unrest. The state representative of the district, one of Weber's men, was reported in the newspaper as

an uncultured Negro, who cannot read or write. He attended during the trouble here a church in Point Coupee, where a colored minister of the African Methodist Church was preaching. He thought it a good occasion to explain his views on the split in the colored ranks, to which the minister objected, saying that the Lord's house was a house of prayer, and not a political clubhouse, but that if the representative wanted to speak about religion he would be gladly heard, whereas if he insisted on talking politics he would be put out. Then the representative to the state legislature arose in wrath and, taking off his coat, challenged the whole congregation to fight. The minister persuaded him to retire, and he went away, but that night the meeting-house was burned down, and nobody doubts that it was done either by himself or through his agency. The

Weber party tried to spread through the parishes the belief that white men burned it down through hatred to the Negro, but that delusion is now dead and will scare no more. The irreconcilable conflict of the races is a lie of the most damnable complexion; was never true; will never be true; and was the invention of Northern Democrats for political purposes.

Weber apparently wasn't about to give up. In October, the feud culminated in an assassination attempt against John Gair, the independent Republican candidate for senate, when rifle shots were fired into his buggy as he headed out of West Feliciana toward Jackson. The rifle ball grazed the back of his companion's neck and struck Gair on the left side of the head, leaving a bad wound. When Weber and armed goons from Bayou Sara arrived in Jackson to patrol the streets and make disparaging remarks about Gair, a riot ensued, during which, the newspaper accounts report, "seven colored men, one horse and one mule were shot."

Another newspaper dispatch in October of 1874 reported optimistically that the "recent difficulties in Bayou Sara" showed encouraging trends for some African American, "though their votes have been largely used to sustain corrupt men, both black and white," to side with

honesty, ready to fight the thieves with arms and with votes. Again, this class are seen to receive the active cooperation of the whites, both Republicans and Democrats, and the conservative influences of property and character—the two great safeguards of free government—are shown to be strong among a considerable number of all classes of the community, strong enough in point of fact to win a decisive victory. So far as this is true, or can be made true of the whole state, Louisiana will prosper. And we may add that this is absolutely the only way in which prosperity can ever be established.

Prosperity and peace would be a long time coming in postwar Louisiana. By March of 1877, Weber's brother, the tax collector, had been murdered in St. Francisville by shots fired from the courthouse lawn. Weber released a statement denying reports that his brother had been going about the streets with a double-barrel shotgun on his shoulder threatening the citizens. Warring factions vied for the statehouse and all the political patronage it controlled, and in the country lawless white "regulators" rode the roads at night intimidating and lynching as they went. John Gair, who survived an earlier assassination attempt, was arrested on a false charge, captured from the sheriff's posse, and murdered by a mob. The newspaper report stated that his major offense, as a black man, was that "he was a man of influence among his people and used his influence for the Republican Party. He was accused of poisoning a citizen. That citizen still lives. But Gair's body, which was riddled with bullets, lies buried in its martyr's grave. Nor his body only. His sister was hanged on the same charge. She, too, had offended the bandits by espousing the Republican cause."

By 1890 there was still unrest. Newspaper accounts report:

> The good citizens of Bayou Sara are mourning over another crime which has been committed in their midst. On Tuesday night a mob of masked men broke open the jail and took therefrom a colored man known as Henry Ward, who had been incarcerated therein for murdering a white man named Benson, from Iowa, an employee of French's circus. A rope was fitted around Ward's neck, the other end thrown over the limb of a tree which was in the Courthouse yard, and Ward was soon swinging twixt heaven and earth. The mob, after pinning to his coat tail a warning to one Harry Brown, another negro, and a mob of negroes who infest Sam Rab's barroom, dispersed. A coroner's jury was impaneled the next day, who in the vain endeavor to obtain a clue to the lynchers, summoned before them all the merchants of the neighborhood, and questioned them closely as to ropes, etc., which they might have sold during the past day. Failing to obtain any evidence, they were compelled to bring in the usual verdict, "Came to his death by strangulation at the hands of unknown parties."

In 1892, area newspapers carried the account of a fatal confrontation by the Freyhan & Co. store.

> Edgar Hamilton, a young white man and two colored men named Rucker, were shot and killed; and Messrs. Wm. Stewart and Bat Haralson were wounded, the former severely and the latter slightly in an affray, at Freyhan & Co's., upper store, St. Francisville. The two Rucker brothers had been arrested for disturbing the peace, and were about to be conveyed to the magistrate's court when they began firing upon the constable, Mr. Geo. Town and several others who were with him. A general fusillade ensued with the above result.

10

Social Life

Author Beulah Smith Watts, who lived on Solitude Plantation just upriver from the port of Bayou Sara, recorded her vivid recollections in the book *Bayou Sara, 1900-1975: Then and Now.* Born in 1894, she remembered visits to the port when she was as young as six, recalling that after its wild and wooly beginnings, Bayou Sara had

quieted down to a very nice and pretty town. There was a lovely hotel managed by Mrs. Burton right near the river front. She had two sons, Wilson and Oren. Later Mrs. Curtain took over management of the hotel. Joe Mayer also had a hotel. John F. Irvine had a beautiful two-story home, wife and two daughters, Frances and Theresa. There were no schools in Bayou Sara. John F. Irvine (Johnnie as he was called) had a big saw mill; there were two saw mills, one was called "The Black Cat." There was a fish market owned by Jack Fields and his wife Elsie. There was a restaurant in connection where excellent fish dinners were served. Joe and Abe Stern had a stable in Bayou Sara where they sold horses, mules and buggies; they also sold harness, saddles and equipment for the farmer; adjoining this was a grocery store and dry goods combined. This store and stable were located at the foot of the Hill from St. Francisville. Across the street from Stern's store was the express office managed by George Plettinger. Mr. Plettinger and his wife, fondly known as 'Miss Anna,' lived with their five children. Mr. Harris also had a store near Stern's store where he sold ladies apparel, men's clothing and groceries. There was also a railroad station where the old "Accommodation" ran from Woodville, Mississippi, to Slaughter, Louisiana. This railroad was just below the hill from St. Francisville.

As a young girl she recalls lots of excitement in Bayou Sara, especially the showboats that tied up to present shows received by culture-starved residents with noisy approval, however primitive the acting. Sometimes there were fundraisers aboard steamers like the *Edward J. Gay,* which in 1881 offered "Grand Moonlight Excursion and Entertainment" with music and refreshments for the benefit of the Catholic Church; tickets were fifty cents. On February 18, 1887, the ladies of the Bayou Sara WCTU (Women's Christian Temperance Union) gave an entertainment the newspaper announcement called

> a drama called "The Social Glass," followed by children's operetta "Prince Puss in Boots." Instrumental and vocal music. All to conclude with a grand dance. Admission for adults, 50c, children half price. They have made arrangements with the *Cleveland* to bring all passengers to the entertainment from Waterloo for 50c, the round trip. The boat passes Waterloo at 4 o'clock on Friday evening and leaves Bayou Sara at 7 next morning.

The same edition of the newspaper carried advice from Bayou Sara's Picard family regarding commerce: "War! War! There are prospects of a war between Germany and France, which will undoubtedly cause all goods to advance in price; we would therefore advise our many customers to call early and supply themselves. A warning to the wise is sufficient."

In June 1887 the WCTU group of Bayou Sara ladies gave another "Grand Dramatic Entertainment at Freyhan's Hall to be followed by a dance. Refreshments will be sold in the hall. Admission for adults 50c and for children 25c. Mr. Irvine's steam ferry will cross passengers from Pointe Coupee who wish to attend the entertainment for 20c. for the round trip, bringing them back the same night. Those who attend can expect to have a nice time." The newspaper noted, "Those who attend can expect to get more than the worth of their money in pleasure, and they will have the consciousness of spending their money in a good cause." That same group, however, was giving some (especially male journalists, apparently) cause for concern, as evidenced in a newspaper snippet in August 1887: "The WCTU is steadily being honey-combed by woman suffrage ideas and rapidly growing into a woman's rights organization, at least to some of the leading female rights champions. Miss Willard, 'Madam President,' is now a suffragist."

"About once a year a giant show boat, Bryant's Floating Palace, docked at Bayou Sara and presented nightly shows with its orchestra. A calliope announced its arrival. You could hear its organ-like whistle for miles around," Mrs. Watts recalled. And in 1913 *The True Democrat* ran an advertisement for W. R. Markle's Golden Rod Floating Theatre coming to Bayou Sara on October 4, "with the Greatest All Feature Show and the Most Expensive Ever Shown Here: 4 shows combined; Thos. A. Edison's Genuine Talking Pictures, His Latest and Most Interesting Invention, Applauded by Millions Throughout the World, Brought Right to Your Door." Other features at the Golden Rod Floating Theatre included "House of Trouble," described as "a quick action Farce Comedy, the kind full of pure fun and sure to make you laugh," plus "6-All Star Vaudeville Acts, The kind that will make you sit up and take notice—all right off the Big City Times," and "Weldon and his Big City Band of 16 pieces, Prof. Aug. Smith's 16-piece Concert Orchestra." As if all that were not enough, the ad touted "Watch for Big Street Parade," and promised "The last and best show of the season" for prices of 25 cents, 35 cents, and 50 cents.

W.W. Cole's Exposition promised Bayou Sara (only two performances, on its fifth tour of the continent)

> the New and Greatest Show on Earth, Zoological and Equestrian! A Mammoth Museum; a Congress of Bewildering Attractions, 10,000 separate and distinct novelties: The Earth, The Sea, The Sky are all represented in a Vast Wilderness of Exhibition Tents; the Most Famous of Family Socials, a Panoply of Splendor; Funny Clowns; 100 Performers having no Equals.

Even the introduction of new steamboats to the river trade occasioned celebrations; 1884 newspapers mentioned the grand reception that was given at Bayou Sara for "the new and splendid steamer *City of Bayou Sara*, of the St. Louis and New Orleans Anchor Line."

Crowds gathered to cheer on the Bayou Sara baseball team as it played teams from the other side of the Mississippi, and the Bayou Sara steam ferry provided transportation across the river for fans at the cut rate of fifty cents for gentlemen and ladies free. Besides the baseball fields, there were fairgrounds with a big pavilion for dancing all day and early evening. Organized in the 1880s, the West Feliciana Fair Association always put on a good show, including horseraces, mule races, wheelbarrow races, as well as culinary and needlework competitions. The Bayou Sara racetrack attracted large crowds from neighboring towns and parishes, and races were often followed by grand balls at Freyhan Hall.

One grand entertainment recorded in April of 1893 was a benefit for the Catholic Church, which consisted of the operatta "R.E. Porter, or The Interviewer and the Fairies," followed by a fine supper and dance at Freyhan Opera House; admission was only fifty cents and "for a noble purpose." That same month a "Grand Concert and Dance" was given for the benefit of the exhibit at the World's Fair and of the Bayou Sara levee fund; admission was fifty cents for a program of "talent furnished by home ama-

Model Ts and other vintage vehicles pass along Royal St. on the way to the fair in Bayou Sara; at left is Propinquity, built in 1809 by Bayou Sara's founder John Mills and later home to German immigrant Dietrich Holl and his nephew Max Nuebling. Courtesy of the West Feliciana Historical Society.

teurs and some of the best talent from Baton Rouge," with special reduced hotel and steamboat rates for the occasion.

Mrs. Watts recalls that the Fairgrounds pavilion was popular for dances as well during the annual fair. "Music was furnished by several bands during the week—Bud Scott from Natchez, Mississippi, Claiburn Williams from Donaldsonville, Louisiana, and Toot Johnson." There were also booths displaying jams, jellies, preserves, pickles, cakes, pies, and canned vegetables in glass jars. Prizes were given, Mrs. Watts recalled, for the most excellent pieced quilts, and embroidered linens were also on display.

There were official visits of warships to all the little towns along the Mississippi, including one in March of 1881 of the *Alliance*, called by the Pointe Coupee *Banner* "one of Uncle Sam's war dogs . . . a neat piece of naval architecture [that] carries six guns." In 1909 the *True Democrat* reported the excitement occasioned by a visit from the president of the United States, with crowds on the Bayou Sara levee cheering the river pageant that went on all afternoon on Saturday, October 30. First four torpedo boats passed down the river, followed by the steamer *Sarah Edenborn* towing barges loaded with Pullman cars, brilliantly lighted. Then came the steamer *Oleander* with President Taft standing at the railing, pausing at the bank for an introduction by Governor Sanders and a twenty-one-gun salute. Eleven steamboats followed.

Social organizations like the IFFs (In For Funs) of Bayou Sara in the 1890s were said to be "composed of the flower of the youthful element of Bayou Sara and St. Francisville" and hosted balls and other events. The Bayou Sara Band in the 1890s played for dances at homes and halls, their "sweet strains much enjoyed by many of the society young folk." In 1899 social items in the papers called the Bayou Sara String Band "peerless."

∞

Once a year, Mrs. Watts remembered, Ringling Brothers Circus came to Bayou Sara, and the school children would rush to watch them unload. Of course, school closed for the day of the circus to give country children the rare opportunity to see the exciting creation of that great American showman, Phineas Taylor Barnum, who had built an exuberant career around exhibiting freaks and frauds (Fee-Gee Mermaids and Siamese twins, giants and midgets, and everything in between), in various museums and theatrical settings until he founded what would become the Ringling Bros. Barnum & Bailey Circus. His original, outrageous autobiography, *The Life of P.T. Barnum written by Himself,* was published in 1855 and gives an amusing account of his troupe's visit to Bayou Sara in 1838.

Barnum's traveling company performed throughout the South that year, from Nashville, where they visited Andrew Jackson, to Vicksburg, Natchez, and St. Francisville. There, a drunk trying to sneak into the tent was denied admission and consequently took aim at Barnum with "a slung-shot." Said Barnum with characteristic colorfulness, "The blow mashed my hat, and grazed the protuberance where phrenologists located the organ of caution." The rejected party returned with "a frightful gang of his half-drunken companions, each with a pistol, bludgeon, or other weapon. They seemed determined to assault me forthwith," Barnum related. The showman begged the mayor and other respectable citizens for protection against the mob, but the mayor "declared his inability to afford it against such odds." The rabble-rouser gave Barnum just one hour to load up his exhibits, strike the tent, and head on downriver on his steamboat. "*He* looked at his watch, *I* looked at the pistols and bludgeons, and I reckon that a big tent never came down with greater speed," said Barnum.

∞

In 1894 a group of performers called the Bayou Sara Minstrel Club performed all over the area. One performance they put on across the Mis-

Members of Bayou Sara Lodge, Knights of Pythias No. 15, shown in March 1896, were commended for playing prominent parts in promoting public welfare. Courtesy of the West Feliciana Historical Society.

sissippi River, written up in the Pointe Coupee *Banner*, featured "Mr. Dreyfus the general manager who acted as interlocutor, and Messrs. Tony Cazedessus, Willie Lawson, George Rettig and J.P. Austin . . . Mr. Cazedessus being especially good in his Irish specialties and local hits." The performance kept the house in a constant roar, especially Revel Matthews

> as Rev. Whangdoodle Baxter in the negro church sketch . . . very realistic and together with his congregation made it plainly evident that they had been there before. This feature of the programme was highly enjoyed by the audience. In the afterplay our old friend Phillip Rettig took off scalps with a deftness that was truly artistic and revealed the master hand. The orchestra which contained such good musicians as our old townsman John Lejeune, the Rettig Brothers, Revel Matthews and Dan Sterling rendered very select music and greatly delighted the audience.

The performance, enhanced by Misses Rettig and Plettinger on piano and violin to augment the gentlemen's performances on banjo, mandolin, and guitar, was over at 12, and followed by a benefit ball for the C.R. of A.

A resolution published in the Bayou Sara *True Democrat* as well as the *Banner* following the performance commended the group for its generosity, saying that "by this generous deed the Bayou Sara Amateur Minstrel Club has not only aided a good and worthy cause, but that it has demonstrated that the object of the organization is not the making of money, but rather to afford pleasure and social and moral entertainment to the people."

11

Crossing the River

The historic little towns of Bayou Sara/St. Francisville and New Roads have been separated over the years by many factors, including culture, language, landscape, and crop differences, but perhaps most evidently by the mighty Mississippi River itself. New Roads, on the west side, was built along False River, an oxbow lake formed when the Mississippi River took a shortcut and cut off a twenty-two-mile curve in its channel. One of the first permanent settlements in the Mississippi Valley, the area had a church by 1738. By the nineteenth century New Roads was predominantly French, with a flat landscape dominated by sugarcane fields. St. Francisville was Anglo and hilly, and cotton was the main cash crop.

And yet, over the years, the two communities have been inextricably bound together as well, beginning in the late 1700s when Capuchin monks from flood-prone Pointe Coupee had to cross the river to the high bluffs of St. Francisville to bury their dead safe from flood waters.

For many years the river crossing was by small ferry, often a tiny tug pushing a barge with limited capacity. Once cars were common, they were packed on so tightly that had the barge sunk, the drivers could not have opened their doors to escape. After the big flood of 1927, the ferry landing was about the only thing left in Bayou Sara with vehicles traversing a narrow roadway down the hill from St. Francisville to catch the ferry that became part of the state highway system. When the river was running high or at flood stage, water pushed onto the low-lying lands all along that thoroughfare.

∞

In 2006 ground was broken to begin construction of a beautiful new bridge, the country's longest cable-stayed structure, which now connects the two communities across the waters of the Mississippi. The approach avenues to the Audubon Bridge have been named in commemoration of something else the two towns have in common—native sons who valiantly served their country in the wars of different generations and rose to the highest rank (commandants) of their chosen branch of service—the U.S. Marine Corps.

The west approach to the bridge was named the General John A. LeJeune Memorial Approach by the state Department of Transportation and Development. Born in 1867 in Pointe Coupee, LeJeune graduated from LSU and the U.S. Naval Academy. During the Spanish-American War he commanded the Marine Guard on the *USS Cincinnati* and *USS Massachusetts*. As he rose through the ranks, he served all over the world, from Norfolk to Panama, Washington, D.C., to the Philippines, and Guantanamo Bay to Vera Cruz.

By the outbreak of World War I, LeJeune was a brigadier general, in command of marine divisions overseas. He would be the first marine officer to hold an Army divisional command when he led the famous Second Division; after the armistice, he led his division in the march into Germany. In 1919 he was appointed commanding general of the marine barracks in Quantico, Virginia, and became the thirteenth commandant of the Marine Corps in 1920. After two terms he retired to serve as superintendent of the Virginia Military Institute. General LeJeune, an active-duty marine for more than forty years, was called "the greatest of all Leathernecks" and received many military honors recognizing his distinguished service (Camp LeJeune in North Carolina bears his name). He was buried in Arlington National Cemetery in 1942.

The bridge approach on the St. Francisville (east) side of the river salutes native son General Robert Hilliard Barrow, twenty-seventh commandant of the Marine Corps, who served in World War II, the Korean War, and the Vietnam War. When General Barrow died at age eighty-six in 2008, *The New York Times* said he "combined Southern courtliness, fierce devotion to Marine tradition and courage reflected in dozens of wars." During the course of his military career, he received the Navy Cross for service in Korea and the Army Distinguished Service Cross in Vietnam, both second only to the Medal of Honor.

Born in 1922, Barrow was raised on his family plantation, Rosale, in West Feliciana Parish, and attended LSU, enlisting in the Marine Corps in March 1942. After being commissioned a second lieutenant in 1943, he was deployed to China and led an American team fighting with Chinese guerrillas extensively in enemy-occupied territory behind Japanese lines. As rifle company commander in the Korean War, he was called the most outstanding company commander of the war. During Vietnam he commanded the Ninth Marine Regiment, Third Marine Division, and was again recognized as the war's finest regimental commander.

After seven tours of duty in the Far East, in 1979 General Barrow became commandant of the Marine Corps, and he was instrumental in implementing much-needed reforms in recruiting and training. He also expanded the marine role in the military's new rapid response strategy. When he retired from the service in 1983, Barrow returned to his beloved home near St. Francisville, and when he died, he opted for burial not in Arlington National Cemetery but in the peaceful oak-shaded cemetery surrounding historic Grace Episcopal Church, which his family had attended for some five generations.

∽

In the early years it was no picnic crossing the Mighty Mississippi. In 1830, according to extensive research conducted by Virginia Lobdell Jennings, the legislature granted Stephen Vanwickle and his heirs "the privilege of operating a ferry across the Mississippi from Bayou Sara to Pointe Coupee for ten years." The ferry, which could be propelled by either steam or horse power, was to start operation by January 1833. With a capacity for two four-wheel carriages, six horses, and twelve passengers in the cabin, the ferry was allowed to charge as follows for crossings:

The sidewheel packet *City of Bayou Sara* was built in Indiana in 1884 and burned at New Madrid, Missouri, in 1885 with the loss of eight lives. Courtesy of Murphy Library Special Collections, University of Wisconsin–La Crosse.

loaded wagon and team: $1.50;
empty wagon: $1;
loaded cart: $1;
empty cart: .37 ½ cents;
gig and horse: $1;
four-wheel carriage and two horses: $2;
man and horse: 75 cents;
single foot passenger: 25 cents;
every head of horned cattle: 37 ½ cents;
every head of sheep or hogs: 18 ¾ cents;
every mule and horse without rider: .25 ¼ cents.

By 1860, New Orleans newspaperman J. W. Dorr recorded that "a good steam ferryboat plies across the river to Pointe Coupee and ought to be a paying institution, for passengers are charged fifty cents each for the luxury of riding over on it, and two dollars if they have a horse and buggy."

Advertisements in the Pointe Coupee *Banner* in 1881 tout Capt. B.T. White's steam ferry making trips from Bayou Sara to Pointe Coupee; White promised the ferry "will answer hails at all hours." The good captain continued in the ferry business for several years at least, as noted in the same newspaper in 1884 referencing him as "Capt. B.T. White, the whole-souled commander of the Bayou Sara Ferry." Boat captains, those skilled pilots who guided their vessels up and down and across the often treacherous waters of the Mississippi River, were held in high esteem. One newspaper account from 1885, for example, described the marriage of Capt. H. W. Pennywitt of the steamer *Morning Star* to Miss Mary Homrich of Bayou Sara, saying, "Capt. Pennywitt is well known to nearly every person living along the banks of the Mississippi from Bayou Sara to Donaldsonville, and we can safely say that a more courteous or popular commander never trod the deck of a steamer."

And in 1890, Captain A. B. French, "the popular showman" whose "New Sensation" was called "by long odds the most conscientious and best show on the river," was accorded a debt of deepest gratitude, according to newspaper accounts, for providing his showboat to transport urgently needed lumber and material to shore up a levee upriver while his show was at Bayou Sara, free of charge and "putting himself to immense trouble and at some expense, and even damaging his staunch little steamer in endeavoring to land between the two levees." Captain French also gave a benefit show with proceeds going toward the upholding of the levee.

Bigstripe inmates load lumber, hogsheads of sugar, and produce onto the steamboat *America* at the Angola landing in 1910. Collection of Louisiana State Penitentiary.

An 1885 newspaper reported in detail a meeting of Bayou Sara's city council that declared the charter or lease of "the privilege of the ferry between Bayou Sara and Pointe Coupee" null and void, with the mayor authorized to receive proposals for a steam ferry. "A movement is on foot among the merchants of Bayou Sara," the account continued, "by which a good and substantial Steam Ferry will be established and one or two trips a day will be made free to the citizens of Pointe Coupee and adjoining parishes who have local business in Bayou Sara. Until a new lease goes into effect, any one has the right to cross passengers and freight and charge their own rates, and no one can interfere with them."

By August of 1885 the newspapers were running a notice that the Bayou Sara steam ferry *Harris Irvine*, recently purchased by Capt. John F. Irvine, would be making "regular trips, promptly answer all hails. Round trip tickets for passengers when numbering ten or more Twenty-five cents." Complaints were being published in the fall of that year, however, because of the lack of shelter provided for passengers and/or their horses. Pointe

Coupee, the local newspaper for the New Roads side of the river reported, "had surrendered its rights in regard to this ferry on condition that this shelter should be immediately provided. This was nearly one year ago, and we are still waiting."

∽

Skip forward half a century to the 1930s, and we find Phillip Morris Bennett Sr. operating a ferry system, privately owned, at Melville on the west side of the river that consisted of two old tugs, *The Melville* and *The Red Cross*, with a wooden barge to hold the few cars wanting to cross. In 1937 Bennett moved to the foot of the hill below St. Francisville by Bayou Sara within close distance of the Mississippi and operated the same two tugs and barge. His son Morris recalls the family hitting town with "an old Model A and a carload of kids. We all worked, and I was the one who helped on the ferry."

A one-car barge propelled by a small attached boat provided ferry service across the Mississippi River from Bayou Sara, ca. 1919. Courtesy of the West Feliciana Historical Society.

Early primitive ferries transported vehicles across the Mississippi between West Feliciana Parish on the east side and Pointe Coupee Parish on the west. Courtesy of the West Feliciana Historical Society.

The old barge held nine cars at a time, and on the average day, only about twenty cars crossed. The leaky old vessels required two pumps, and Morris Bennett recalls "spending half my life sitting on a pitcher pump, pumping water out when the oakum came loose from the seams." He was all of five years old when he first took to the water, helping his father and even spending nights on the boat. By the age of eleven or twelve, he was running the ferry vessel himself, and in 1945, still in high school, he became a licensed ferry pilot, working eight-hour shifts on the ferry; one teacher used to let him sleep in class, knowing he needed rest.

Left and below: The old *Red Cross*
ferry, shown in the 1930s, was a
30-hp cypress boat operated by
generations of the Bennett family. Courtesy of the West Feliciana
Historical Society.

Ferry captain P. Morris Bennett Sr. operated the Mississippi River ferry at Bayou Sara from the 1930s until he retired and let his son Morris Jr., who first took to the water at age five helping his father, take over. Courtesy of the West Feliciana Historical Society.

Morris Jr. loved the river and everything on it, saying,

At age 16 I could tell every steamboat on the Mississippi just by the whistle. The *Seminole* had the prettiest whistle on the river. That Standard Oil's *D.R. Willow*, too, and the *Jack Rathbone* had the prettiest lines. The *Sprague*, which everybody used to call 'Big Mama,' looked just like a floating castle; she was another Standard Oil boat. I'd wait ten minutes to get out on the river after that one, she cast such a big wake. In the 1927 high water the U.S. government asked Standard Oil to dock the *Sprague;* the huge waves from it were breaking up the levees. I'd get a lot of information from those old steamboat pilots.

Licensed ferry pilots Captains P. Morris Bennett senior and junior operated a variety of ferryboats crossing the Mississippi River from the Bayou Sara landing for more than half a century beginning in the 1930s. Courtesy of the West Feliciana Historical Society.

He eventually took over for his father when Captain Bennett Sr. retired after nearly half a century on the river—a tenure Morris himself would match. When Captain Bennett Sr. retired, he could still be seen along the banks checking the river gauge on most days, and now that Morris has retired, he too checks on the river most days.

And boy, can he tell some tales. "I've done everything but deliver a baby," he laughs, "and I've come close to doing that twice. Only things I won't cross are a pregnant mule and a one-eyed goat!" But with only those exceptions, he ferried everything else imaginable across the Mississippi between Bayou Sara/St. Francisville and New Roads, including elephants and monkeys, run-away boars, midstream motorcycle weddings, and moonshiners and revenuers, and he has crossed through hurricanes, ice floes, fires, and earthquakes. "We nearly had a funeral, but I sent them to Angola's ferry to scatter the ashes there instead, since we've got too much traffic here. You name it, we've seen it!"

Morris's years on the river were exciting ones. In 1939 the river was almost completely frozen for nine days, and he could stand out in the middle of the Mississippi. Bayou Sara creek froze completely over, and the ice in the river floes was six to eight feet deep. One time, in the dead of winter, the tug lost a propeller. Said Morris, "We couldn't get it anywhere to be fixed, so Daddy and another hand got overboard to fix it. They had a fifth sitting on the stern and would come up to get a little warmth. They both about froze to death. Afterwards we had to wrap them up in layers of quilts. I sat on the back steps crying, I was so sure Daddy was dying."

More recent ferries had over one thousand-horsepower with backups and lots of radar, radios, and equipment rather than just the compass on early ones. In the early days, with just a thirty-horsepower Fairbanks Morse CO_2 engine, strong winds or squalls would catch the ferry and set it drifting. "Once we got caught in a squall," Morris recalls, "and blown down to the bend. We had to stop there. Old Dave Gray was working with me, and he threw a 250-pound anchor onto the sandbar to hold us there. When we were ready to try to get back, he couldn't move that anchor alone. He didn't know his own strength when his adrenaline was pumping."

It was a real community service, running the ferry crossing.

Folks would start blowing their horn coming down the hill from St. Francisville to the landing at Bayou Sara so we'd wait for them. In the 1950s the state took over ownership of the ferries and the Police Jury was supposed to maintain the ferry ramps but never did much, so when the river fell after a flood there'd sometimes be four feet of silt left, and we'd

In the 1950s the state of Louisiana took over ownership of the Mississippi River ferries, after years of private operation. Courtesy of the West Feliciana Historical Society.

have to shovel it off and make a mat of willow poles with planks on top so cars could drive down to board the ferry.

The hill down to the ferry landing was steep when the river was low, and Captain Bennett recalls one fully loaded gravel truck somehow slipping into neutral trying to change gears for the descent; the driver just jumped out onto the ferry deck, and that truck went straight on through, across the deck and into the river.

"Times have really changed," said Morris.

Those were the good old days. We'd make trips after hours in any emergency; people would just come to us to help, and we did. In the 1946 hurricane, the one that killed a couple hundred people and then came up the river, the sheriff threatened to put us in jail to keep us safe, but we rode out that storm in the ferry boat to look out for it. We were doing fine until the eye of the storm passed over and the wind shifted. The water swamped us. There was water in the wheel house, and we couldn't swim for all of it. The waves just washed us out on the bank and we crawled out and held onto some willows. The next day we saw the barge 10 or 12 feet up on the bank.

But the most fascinating thing I ever saw on the river was the Alaska earthquake. It was about 12:30 or 1 a.m., and I felt the boat surge twice. I looked out, and there was no boat passing. I said "Something's not right here." I looked over to the bank, and the whole ramp was wet. That river had just tilted! There was about a 15-degree angle on the ramp, and I measured where the water had gone up it 43 feet.

Bennett calls the river "the hottest place in the world in the summer and the coldest place in winter. I used to hug that old kerosene stove. We used to have a four-car barge, and we had to squeeze the fourth car on by bouncing the third car over. No way they could have opened their doors if the ferry went down. We got a one-piece ferry while I was in military service, with outboard engines at first." More recent ferries, *The St. Francisville* and *The New Roads* (identical boats) had forty-car capacities and were operated twenty-four hours a day, in good weather and bad, crossing 1,100 to 1,200 cars a day before the bridge opened.

Almost as unpredictable as the weather, and just as dangerous, were the many and varied animals Captain Bennett ferried.

Once an old Model A chicken truck, loaded down with crates of chickens, drove on. Those old trucks had the gas opening up by the windshield, and this one must have lost its cap. It was hot, and you could see the fumes coming up out of the gas tank. The old fellow driving the truck got out and stood up by the hood and struck a match to light up a big old cigar. Man, was there an explosion! We were about 75 feet from the bank at that point, so we started back. We just had water buckets to fight fires with then, like we just had cypress boards for life preservers. The boat railing caught on fire, and so did the truck driver, who jumped overboard. We used a long spike pole to pull crates of chickens off the truck. The smell of burning feathers was something awful! The live chickens escaped on the levee, and I sure did get tired of eating chicken after that. Every time Daddy reached for an ear of corn, I knew we'd be having chicken that night!

In high water we'd try to help the cattlemen out by going out to Cat Island to evacuate the cattle out of the flooded swamp on the ferry. I remember Mr. Ewell Mahoney had a four-star bull, and we went three days trying to get him out. He was standing in a foot of water by then. Whitty and Eugene Young finally got a rope on the bull, but he broke away. Daddy and I were in a pirogue and grabbed the flying end of the rope. That bull wheeled around and got in that pirogue with us! Man, you talk about somebody shinny up a cypress tree! We'd get plenty of game then, during high water in the swamps. We didn't have any trouble keeping the table stocked with ducks, and rabbits were so thick you could just hit them with a stick.

I even had elephants cross on the ferry. Whole circuses used to cross that way. Their old trucks couldn't pull the grade on the ramp, so they'd unload the elephants to push them up the hill. Then there was the time somebody came on board with a monkey they'd just bought for their son. He was a bad little boy, just awful, and pretty soon that monkey got loose. It climbed up to the pilothouse where Daddy was, and it was a standoff between him and that monkey for awhile!

Once a pregnant Oriental lady crossed and got out to sit on the bow with a cat. She was holding that cat and loving it. After we docked, she and her husband drove up the ramp and parked. We went on across the river. They were still sitting there when we docked again, and here came the husband running down to the river with that cat, the wife running after him. He slung that cat as far as he could out into the water, then he got out in the water himself and tried to keep it from swimming to shore. Finally the cat made a big semicircle and got back to the bank. Turned out the cat had used the car for a bathroom.

The ferry's old metal deck was hot as blazes. One day two old men in a beat-up pickup drove on, the sides of the truck just falling apart. In the bed of the pickup was a big old hog, laid down and tied with old rotten ropes. That hog smelled the water and here he came! He burst those rotten ropes and hit the back gate. The whole thing was coming off. Those two old men jumped up and threw it back, shouting 'Heave!' That hog would hit the back again, and they'd shout 'Heave!' and push it back. I got worried; I had a bunch of people on board and didn't need that big hog loose. Finally I saw somebody with a good lasso and we tied that hog up tight. Hogs don't have sweat glands, you know; that's why they wallow in mud. Sometimes I'd wet them down with the firehose to cool them off, crossing on hot days. Another time a whole truckload of cattle got loose on the landing. I think the trailer gate opened just as they were about to drive the load onto the ferry.

If the weather and the animals gave some anxious but humorous moments to the ferry captain, consider the people:

The bootleggers would cross late at night, and would always wait until we blew the whistle and were about to pull out before they'd board, to make sure the revenuers weren't aboard. They drove old Chevy or Ford trucks with chicken crates in the back to make it look legitimate. One old fellow carried around the same chicken so long that all its feathers fell off. The revenuers used to ride the ferry all night long trying to catch them.

Even after the demise of the little port city of Bayou Sara, the ferry landing there saw plenty of action—at least until the traffic moved south to cross the Mississippi on the Audubon Bridge. But the steamboats still dock at Bayou Sara, their passengers boarding buses for the trip up the hill into historic downtown St. Francisville atop the bluff. And, visitors coming down the hill from St. Francisville might see a four-wheel ATV, American flag flying from its rear, descending the hill from St. Francisville to the water's edge. And in the driver's seat, sunglasses protecting diminished vision, is that old ferry pilot Morris Bennett coming to check on the river level as he does on a daily basis. It's that river water he's got in his veins drawing him back to its source, and if the visitors are especially lucky and he's in a talkative, friendly mood—as he usually is, man, can he tell some stories.

Morris Bennett Jr. driving his golf cart down to the river in his old age with the *Queen of the Mississippi* steamboat in the background. Courtesy of Derry Anne Bennett Cartee.

Used To Be

Visitors today should drive along St. Francisville's main street, Ferdinand, past the Victorian cottages and stepped brick storefronts and historic churches, and down the steep hill toward the Mississippi River. All they'll see now are a few structures raised on piers and the Corps of Engineers Mat Field where they make the big concrete mats to line riverbanks and levees to prevent erosion.

There used to be an important port city here, Bayou Sara, its squares filled with noisy saloons and bustling emporiums where the shopkeeps put their inventories on the highest shelves to keep doing business when the streets and stores were flooded.

There used to be fine homes and a church with an upstairs gallery that provided a refuge when crevasses in the levee let ten or twenty feet of river floodwater rush through town.

There used to be wharves lined with flatboats loaded with produce and goods, then later fancy steamboats like floating palaces and fast packets piled so high with bales of cotton that the boats themselves were hardly visible.

There used to be a ferry landing here, most recently part of the highway system, where the pilots passed skills and river lore down through their families and where they knew generations of passengers crossing from one side of the river to the other and then back again.

Visitors won't see any of those things now. It's all about what used to be. It's not here any more.

Bibliography

"A River Horror." *New Orleans Times Democrat.* December 15, 1886.

Adams, Donna Burge. "Trades and Professions in the Florida Parishes of Louisiana." Baton Rouge, LA: printed by author, 1989.

———. "Fires, Feuds, and Floods in the Florida Parishes of Louisiana." Baton Rouge, LA: printed by author, 1989.

"Amateur Ethiopian Minstrels." *Times-Picayune.* July 13, 1855.

"Another Steamboat Explosion." *Brooklyn Daily Eagle.* October 3, 1843.

Arthur, Stanley C. "The Story of the West Florida Rebellion." *St. Francisville Democrat* (St. Francisville, LA). 1935.

———. *Old Families of Louisiana.* 1931. Reprint, Baton Rouge, LA: Claitor's Publishing Division, 1971.

Barry, John M. *Rising Tide: The Great Mississippi Flood of 1927 and How it Changed America.* New York: Simon & Schuster, 1998.

Bayou Sara Map. New York: Sanborn Map & Publishing Company. May 1885.

Ibid. New York: Sanborn Map & Publishing Company: January 1922.

"Bayou Sara: A Mississippi River Saga." *The Advocate.* July 30, 2007.

"Bayou Sara –As It Was in 1881." *Louisiana Churchman and Industrial News* (Bayou Sara, LA). August 29, 1888.

"Bayou Sara and St. Francisville Are Two Different Towns." *True Democrat* (St. Francisville, LA), March 11, 1976. (Reprinted from Silver Anniversary Edition, 1917).

Bersuder, Robert Nicholas. "A History of *The St. Francisville True Democrat*." PhD diss., Louisiana State University, 1951.

Birmingham, Stephen. *The Grandes Dames*. Boston: G.K. Hall, 1983.

Browning, Robert M. Jr. *Lincoln's Trident: The West Gulf Blockading Squadron During the Civil War*. Tuscaloosa: University of Alabama Press, 2015.

Butler, Anne. "The Day the War Stopped." *St. Francisville Democrat*. June 25, 1998.

———. *Three Generous Generations*. St. Francisville, LA: West Feliciana Historical Society, 2004.

———. *A Tourist's Guide to West Feliciana Parish: A Little Bit of Heaven Right Here on Earth*. Xlibris Corporation, 2001.

Butler, Anne and Henry Cancienne. *Main Streets of Louisiana*. Lafayette, LA: University of Louisiana at Lafayette Press, 2012.

Butler, Anne and Norman C. Ferachi. *St. Francisville and West Feliciana Parish*. Charleston, SC: Arcadia Publishing, 2014.

Butler, Louise. "West Feliciana and a Glimpse of its History." *Louisiana Historical Quarterly* 7, no. 1 (1925): 90.

Carpenter, Almena Kilbourne. "Bayou Sara: Pawn of the Mississippi." *Morning Advocate* (Baton Rouge, LA). November 23, 1952.

Chitty, Darrell and Anne Butler. *Spirit of St. Francisville.* n.p., 2007.

Civil War Navy: A Selection of Excellent Naval Letters. Metairie, LA: The Historical Shop, 2016.

"Conditions Serious at Bayou Sara." *New Orleans Item.* May 1, 1912.

"Congressman Wickliffe Meets Tragic Death at Washington." *True Democrat* (St. Francisville, LA). June 15, 1912.

Dabney, Thomas Ewing. *Revolution or Jobs: The Odenheimer Plan for Guaranteed Employment*. New York: The Dial Press, 1933.

Dart, Elisabeth Kilbourne. "The Printers' Cottage." unpublished memoir, West Feliciana Historical Society, St. Francisville, LA. n.d.

Dorr, J.W. "A Tourist Description of Louisiana, 1860." Edited by Ed. Walter Prichard. *Louisiana Historical Quarterly*, 21 (October 1938): 1,134-36.

"To Have Your Horse's Leg Cleverly Broken . . ." *Feliciana Sentinel* (St. Francisville, LA). December 1, 1877.

"From the Interior." *Times-Picayune.* October 5, 1855.

Harrison, A.W. Letter to West Feliciana Historical Society. November 5, 2005. Gastrell Family History.

Hart, John E. "Commanding the USS Albatross." *Civil War Times Illustrated* 15.4 (July 1976): 28-35.

"History of German-American Relations: 1683-1900-History and Immigration." US State Department IIP publications. June 2008.

"J.M.White." Steamboat Times, A Pictorial History of the Mississippi Steamboating Era. http://steamboattimes.com/index.html.

Jennings, Virginia Lobdell. "Bayou Sara—The Town and Stream." Louisiana Genealogical Register. March 1996. http://www.rootsweb. com/~usgenweb/copyright.htm.

Jennings, Virginia L. *The Plains and the People.* Baton Rouge, LA: Land & Land, 1989.

Karwowski, Francis I. "The Yankee Grave That Dixie Decorates." St. George's Lodge #6 Free and Accepted Masons. http://www. stgeorgeslodge.org/historical/commander-hart/.

"2,000 Men Wanted." *Keystone* (Harrisburg, PA). October 5, 1836.

Lester, C.E. "The Gunboat Essex." *Harper's New Monthly Magazine.* February 1863.

"Louisiana Places: St. Francisville & Bayou Sara." *Sunday Advocate* (Baton Rouge, LA). March 3, 1974.

"Masonic Burial Accorded by Dixie Masons to a Man Who Shelled Town." *The Missouri Consistory: The Official Publication of the Scottish Rite Bodies* (St. Louis, MO). May 1949.

Neubling, Max. Unpublished letters to family in Germany. August 18, 1826. Louisiana State University Special Collections, Baton Rouge, LA.

"*Oleander,* With President Party Aboard, Makes Landing Amid Noisy Welcome." *True Democrat* (St. Francisville, LA). October 30, 1909.

"Organization of the Bayou Sara Compress Company." *Times-Democrat.* Special to *Pointe Coupee Banner* (Bayou Sara, LA) April 6, 1887.

"Overflow at Bayou Sara." *New York Tribune.* July 19, 1844.

Pointe Coupee Democrat (New Roads, LA). April, May, July 1858.

"Recently our Friend Jno F. Irving of Bayou Sara ..." *Feliciana Sentinel* November 6, 1880.

Riffel, Judy. "West Feliciana Parish Business Licenses, 1884-1899." *Le Raconteur* (June 2012): 98-121.

Schafer, W.G. *Records of Bayou Sara, LA 1855-1868.* Unpublished memoir. West Feliciana Historical Society, St. Francisville, LA. 1868.

Silver Anniversary Edition of *The True Democrat* (St. Francisville, LA). February 24, 1917.

Simkin, John. "Immigration to the USA: 1820-1860." Last modified August 2014. http://spartacus-educational.com/USAE1820.htm.

"Southern Cities are Being Flooded." *Dunkirk Evening Observer.* (Dunkirk, NY). May 4, 1912.

"Steamboat Officers Indicted." *Times-Picayune.* June 11, 1851.

Szasz, Ferenc Morton. *Religion in the Modern American West.* Tucson: University of Arizona Press, 2000.

Tenney, Jona. S. Letter to Miss Rebecca Tenney. Apr 27, 1840. Antebellum Louisiana. Center for Arkansas History and Culture,

Little Rock, Arkansas.

"The Country." *Times-Picayune.* September 19, 1865.

"The Great Fire at Bayou Sara." *Times-Picayune.* June 20, 1855.

"The State in Mourning." *Times-Picayune.* March 8, 1859.

Union Army: Cyclopedia of Battles. Madison, WI: Federal Publishing, 1908.

"*USS Essex* (1856)." Wikipedia. https://en.wikipedia.org/wiki/USS_Essex_(1856) January 30, 2016.

Watts, Beulah Smith. *Bayou Sara 1900-1975.* Baton Rouge, LA: Claitor's Publishing Division, 1976.

"West Feliciana Parish Newspapers."West Feliciana Parish LAGenWeb.

West Feliciana Parish, Louisiana, Census Records: 1800s and 1900s.

"W.R. Markle's Golden Rod Floating Theatre (advertisement)." *True Democrat* (St. Francisville, LA). October 4, 1913.

"Yankee Grave Dixie Decorates Reveals Strange Tale." *Times-Picayune.* October 14, 1937.

Index

Printed in the USA
CPSIA information can be obtained
at www.ICGtesting.com
CBHW080704220124
3595CB00006B/19